The Revenue Runway™

Your Ticket to Growing a Business
in the Turbulence of Life

Kalen Marie Cotto

The Revenue Runway™
Your Ticket to Growing a Business in the Turbulence of Life

© 2025 by Kalen Marie Cotto

All rights reserved. No part of this book may be reproduced by any mechanical, photographic, or electronic process, or in the form of a phonographic recording; nor may it be stored in a retrieval system, transmitted, or otherwise be copied for public or private use—other than for "fair use" as brief quotations embodied in articles and reviews—without prior written permission of the publisher.

Design and cover art by Peaceful Profits.

Paperback ISBN: 978-1-967587-64-3
eBook ISBN: 978-1-967587-65-0

Disclaimer: The information contained in this book is provided for educational purposes only and should not be construed as legal, financial, tax, or investment advice. Readers are strongly encouraged to consult with a qualified and licensed professional who can provide advice tailored to their individual circumstances. Laws, regulations, and financial practices vary across countries, states, and regions. Market conditions, returns, and outcomes will differ over time and cannot be guaranteed. While every effort has been made to provide accurate and timely information at the time of writing, we make no representations or warranties regarding completeness, accuracy, or applicability. We are not making any official legal or financial recommendations. The examples, figures, and principles presented herein are for illustrative and educational purposes only. Any decisions you make are solely your responsibility.

Scripture quotations are from the ESV® Bible (The Holy Bible, English Standard Version®), © 2001 by Crossway, a publishing ministry of Good News Publishers. ESV Text Edition: 2025. The ESV text may not be quoted in any publication made available to the public by a Creative Commons license. The ESV may not be translated in whole or in part into any other language. Used by permission. All rights reserved.

Dedicated to my daughter, Kaya, who grew up watching me struggle but reminded me that it would all be worth it in the end. And to my husband, Javy, who pushed me to invest in myself and helps me to be courageous every day.

*The plans of the diligent lead surely to abundance,
but everyone who is hasty comes only to poverty.*
–Proverbs 21:5 (ESV)

Table of Contents

Introduction: Business is Personal vii

Part 1: Why You Need a Revenue Runway 1

    Chapter 1: The Best Businesses Are Built Out of Hard Times 3

    Chapter 2: It's Time to Rescue Yourself 11

    Chapter 3: Let's Be Real 21

    Chapter 4: The Key to It All 55

    Chapter 5: The Problem With Action 65

Part 2: From Roadblocks to the Revenue Runway 73

    Chapter 6: Clear the Way for Clients 75

    Chapter 7.0: Introduction to the 3 Pillars of the Revenue Runway . 79

    Chapter 7.1: Irresistible Offer 83

    Chapter 7.2: Ideal Client Avatar 97

    Chapter 7.3: Solid Sales Strategies 105

Part 3: Blueprints to Your Revenue Runway 119

    Chapter 8: Your Irresistible Offer Blueprint 121

    Chapter 9: Your Ideal Client Avatar 125

    Chapter 10: Your Core Sales Message 137

Conclusion 141

Resources 145

About the Author 147

Introduction
Business Is Personal

Will I really be able to stay on active duty in the Army Reserve with a newborn at home?

It was January 2010, and I was due to give birth to my first child in July. That question kept rolling around in my mind, and I wasn't sure what I was going to do.

At the time, I was serving as the head of public affairs for a command in the Army Reserve that oversaw 22 states. I was able to work from home for a while, but I carried my BlackBerry everywhere I went. It was an intense position, and I was afraid it would require more from me than I could give as a new mom.

I couldn't just quit, though. We needed my income, so I decided to start a side hustle helping small businesses with branding and social media. I had always wanted to have my own business. Why not now?

Honestly, there were a lot of reasons most people would have said it was a horrible time for me to start a business, even if it was only a freelance side hustle.

I was entering a season with a newborn that would bring a significant change to my life. Was this really a good idea? I wasn't sure, but I had to try.

I worked for the Army during the day and on my own business after hours. By the time my maternity leave was over and I went back into the office, people had started noticing what I was doing and were asking for my help. That's when my little side hustle started to grow into something bigger.

The funniest part about starting when I wasn't ready is that my life was about to get even more chaotic, but I didn't know it. My life has proven time and again that there will never be a perfect time to start the thing you have dreamed of doing. But before I get into that, let me introduce myself.

Who I Am

My name is Kalen Marie Cotto, and I built a successful online service provider business while working full-time in the Army Reserve with a new baby. Although that probably sounds crazy, I'm so glad I did it because it proved to me that anyone can build a business during a challenging season of life.

I left my career in the military over a decade ago and have been an entrepreneur ever since. Although running a business is a lot of work, I love what I do. It provides me with the time and financial freedom to live life on my own terms.

How many people can say that today? Not nearly enough! I think everyone who dreams of having their own business should get the chance, ESPECIALLY if everything else seems to be falling apart. I have been helping clients grow their businesses for years. In this book, I'm sharing everything I know.

Why I Wrote This Book

Why would a busy mom with a hectic agency take time out of her life to write a book about how to start a business when life kicks you in the teeth? Three reasons:

- Reason #1: It's not as hard to start or grow a business as you might think. This book will show you that with a proven process and a step-by-step roadmap, it takes less time, effort, and money than you'd imagine. You can build a business in a way that's manageable, so it doesn't feel like you're risking everything to jump off a cliff. There is a proven framework that can help, and I'm going to teach it to you in this book.
- Reason #2: I'm tired of watching people put their dreams on the shelf. If you've always wanted to start a business but are waiting for the perfect time, stop waiting! Life is messy. There's never a good time to start a business. I can show you how to get started quickly so you're not still stuck in neutral and living with regret a year from now.
- Reason #3: Time is the only resource you can't create more of, and entrepreneurship is the best way to enable yourself to spend your time as you wish. While you're spending eight or more hours a day working to help build someone else's business, you're giving your valuable time to someone else's dreams. This is stealing hours, days, weeks, and years from your life. You do NOT have to

settle for that! Instead, this book will help you focus on building your own business one step at a time.

Why You Should Read This Book

Bottom line? The time is now. You're ambitious, and you've wanted to do this for years. You've put your dreams on hold for too long, and now life is staring you in the face demanding that you make something happen. You need a practical guide on how to grow a business when life is kicking your ass!

Maybe you've experienced a career setback. Maybe you're dealing with an illness or an injury. Maybe you just want to spend more time with your kids. Or maybe you already have your own business, but it isn't experiencing the growth you expected. Whatever brought you to this book, I'm not going to send you away empty-handed.

This book contains my step-by-step blueprint for building a business that I call the Revenue Runway™. The Revenue Runway framework will show you exactly what to do at every point in the journey whether you're just starting, you're struggling to grow, or you're ready to scale.

I've taken everything I've learned through trial and error or paying others to help me and put it into a format that can help others avoid spending 12 years making the same mistakes I did.

The Revenue Runway framework helped me stop overthinking and take action, and I'm so glad I did! Because of this framework, I no longer worry about returning to a desk job where my time belongs to someone else. I have the blueprint to continue operating and growing my business no matter what the economy is doing or what's happening in the world.

By the time you finish this book, you'll have a clear understanding of what you want to offer, and you will know the exact steps you need to achieve your goals. This will help you take action with confidence and stick to those actions, even when there are bumps in the journey.

You don't have to do this alone! Throughout this book, I'll share more information about my Revenue Runway program where you can find the training, support, and community you need to start, strengthen, and scale your business.

What's Inside This Book

In part 1 of this book, I'll give you an inside look at why NOW is the best time to start or grow a business and why YOU are the best person to do it, even if (especially if) life is kicking your ass right now. You'll go through a self-assessment that will help you identify any roadblocks in your way, so you can use this book as your guide to overcome them—no matter what's going on in your life.

In part 2, I'll introduce you to the Revenue Runway framework and show you how it is the answer to your question, "How do I start or grow a business during challenging circumstances so I'm not wasting time or money on strategies that don't work?" You'll also learn how to identify whom you want to serve and how you'll serve them. We'll take a look at streamlining your systems and processes so you can take the shortest path possible to closing clients and generating revenue.

Part 3 is where things get really good because you'll find the Revenue Runway classroom and Revenue Runway Blueprint Workbook there. That is where you'll learn how to fix a struggling business and how to scale a business. That's right—this isn't your average read-it-and-forget-it book. You'll have everything you need to start DOING.

Does that sound like a lot? Don't worry, it's all step by step and everything in this book can be summed up in three points:

- Point #1: Life is messy. There is never a good time to start a business. Waiting for the perfect time means you'll never start. Don't wait.
- Point #2: Businesses are built one step at a time at your own speed.
- Point #3: There is a proven framework that can help, and this book will teach it to you.

My goal for you is to have clarity on your offer (the products or services you're selling) and be ready to take action to start or grow your business before you even finish this book. Helping entrepreneurial people like you start and scale their own business in a way that fits the life they want is exactly what I do, and my team and I would love to help you, too.

If you read this book and would like help implementing the information I provide as quickly as possible without having to figure it all out yourself, then book a call to chat with my team by visiting https://therevenuerunway.com.

Business Is Personal

For now, let's dive into chapter 1 where I'm going to explain what the Revenue Runway framework is and how it can change your life.

Part 1

Why You Need a Revenue Runway

Chapter 1

The Best Businesses Are Built Out of Hard Times

Some businesses are started after months or years of planning and groundwork. Others are started out of necessity. If you are reading this book because necessity has led you to the conclusion that you want to start or grow a business: good.

That's right: good! The best businesses are built out of hard times.

Hard times are when we become our most creative, persistent, and tenacious. Being an entrepreneur requires all three qualities, so don't count yourself out just because your life feels upside down or you're dealing with challenges. I want you to know that mountains can be moved with a little creativity, persistence, and tenacity!

It wasn't long ago that I was balancing client work and childcare during a messy divorce. I was desperately trying not to drop any of the balls I was juggling. Honestly, I didn't always succeed. If dealing with hard times disqualifies a person from starting a business, then I'd have never been allowed anywhere near the starting line.

Today, I have a successful business as a digital marketer helping businesses of all kinds grow and scale. How did I build my business when it felt like life was kicking my ass?

I relied on a framework based on proven business principles that helped me build my business one step at a time. I call this framework the Revenue Runway.

Truthfully, I didn't even know it was a framework until I broke down the elements that were working for all of our clients across the board. This book explains each step along the way, and our online resources in part 3 will help you get the jumpstart you need.

What is the Revenue Runway?

The Revenue Runway is a straightforward, step-by-step roadmap for establishing a business. It eliminates the unnecessary fluff and focuses on specific action tasks that help entrepreneurs like you get their businesses up and running (or growing and scaling) in less time and with less stress than you ever imagined!

Many service providers begin by agonizing over what to offer. They waste time on fancy websites, branding, and detailed business plans. Yet none of those things actually put money in your pocket unless you have an offer that clients want and the ability to sell it to them!

The Revenue Runway framework is different. It helps service providers zero in on exactly whom they want to serve, and then figure out how the talents and skills they have can contribute. That way, they can create irresistible offers that are tested and validated to sell before they start marketing anything.

Does This Approach Really Work?

I used the Revenue Runway to build my own business from zero to six figures and learned it piece by piece from high-ticket experts and coaches. It was so effective for me that I started using it with my clients in my digital marketing agency.

Do you want to know what happened? My clients achieved great results too! The Revenue Runway shortened the learning curve, helped them avoid mistakes, and built a faster path to success.

No matter the size of your business or service industry, the Revenue Runway principles are the same—and they work. This book outlines the same process I walk my clients through as they grow and scale. In the past few years, my team and I have helped:

- Restoration cleaning businesses
- Local service businesses
- Environmental attorneys
- Military nonprofit organizations
- Orthodontists
- Life coaches
- Rheumatologists
- Financial planners

And the list keeps growing! This book describes the entire framework and every lesson I learned along the way so you can get started on the Revenue Runway now—without having to pay for high-ticket coaching or mentorship.

What Can the Revenue Runway Framework Do for You?

When you follow the advice in this book, your business (and life) will become more organized and you'll gain better control over the direction of your business. Instead of your business controlling your life, you'll experience more purpose and freedom.

When something goes wrong, you'll be able to quickly identify and fix the problem because you'll have the step-by-step Revenue Runway framework. And those chaotic 14-hour days that startup service providers typically experience? You don't have to experience that. The clear systems you build your business around will protect your time as you serve clients.

Even if you feel like life is beating you up right now, the Revenue Runway framework makes it possible to build a profitable business with the time you have. Let's be honest—life happens! But with a simple step-by-step plan, you CAN do this. Check out these examples of clients that my team and I have helped.

> **Case Study #1: From Referral Drought to Booked Out Orthodontic Practice**
>
> We started working with an orthodontic practice that first learned about us on our old podcast. After listening to every

episode, they booked a phone call and became our client. Although they offered unique services, they were struggling to attract new patients and were surviving on referrals from other dental clinics.

We started by auditing their online presence, and what we found wasn't good. Most of their online platforms were barely being used, and it looked like their locations weren't even open. We began by updating their websites and social media accounts to show activity. Once that was done, we tested and built two sales funnels (websites specifically designed to prompt clients and customers to take a specific action; in this case, generate leads and book appointments) for them to ensure their messaging was attracting the right clients.

Within 30 days of the funnels going live, qualified leads were calling their office and booking appointments. They were receiving twice as many leads and bookings than the standard for that industry. Today, they have two on-demand, lead-generating assets that they can turn on or off to attract new leads that flow in like water from a faucet.

Case Study #2: Estate Trust Service

At first glance, this client seemed to have it all figured out. Honestly, I wasn't sure what was lacking. Their branding was gorgeous. They had a solid offer. They emailed their list weekly. They were featured on prominent podcasts and seemed to be landing sales.

After asking more questions, I realized that they had gotten lucky. One episode of a podcast had provided them with enough web traffic to fill their sales pipeline for almost an entire year! However, they did not have any other mechanisms in place to continue once those leads were fulfilled.

Our team began click testing using Facebook ads right away to determine what ad copy would pull in users immediately. We had verbiage within five days. Within ten days, we had a series of landing pages and tracking on all activity using heat maps and clicks.

The course they were selling consisted of a four-page series of videos on how trusts and estates worked. Within a month, they had over 5,300 people engaged and over 1,400 converting to sales calls.

Case Study #3: Local Frame Shop

This client came to us in a bit of a panic. She had a custom framing business specializing in paintings, memorabilia, and more. By the time we started working together, she had already been in the business for about 20 years.

When COVID hit in 2020, she went from having regular walk-in clients to having no one leave the house. Her phone had almost stopped ringing, and the few who called the shop were afraid to come in. She told me that if she didn't figure something out, she would have to close her doors.

So we explored online options. Her clients could schedule a Zoom call and then drop off items in front of the store for processing. Because her storefront was all windows, she could see outside when people were dropping off an order. She could then leave the finished piece in a drop box for order pickup.

> But how would she make appointments? Her existing website was outdated and only had the business name and a lot of text.
>
> We immediately started on a simple logo and a one-page website with instructions on how to book a call online via Zoom. The website also had a list of materials to choose from for framing, matting, and other options.
>
> We created social media accounts, photographed the entire store, and developed templates for her to use via Canva. This helped her generate ideas and she trained an in-house employee to take it over.
>
> Within weeks of launching, she was fully booked. The cost of our services was recouped by just one job from a client located an hour away. She said the results saved her business. She could not believe that such small changes had such a big impact.

I hope these stories show you how the Revenue Runway is more than just a how-to-build-a-business course. It's a recipe for changing your life and getting you to a place where you have financial freedom and your time is your own.

Bulletproof Truth

Because of the Revenue Runway, I was able to build a business that absolutely changed my life during one of the most challenging periods I've ever experienced. My business allows me to set my own schedule so I can work around my daughter's activities while earning a full-time income. It has also served as a vehicle for me to provide services that I enjoy and am passionate about. And this year, my business made it possible for my now husband and me to buy our dream home during a tough economy.

It's my goal to help more entrepreneurial-minded individuals like you build businesses they love in a proven and sustainable way. It's possible for you, too, no matter what the circumstances of your life are right now.

Here's What's Coming Up Next…

In this book, I break down the nine steps of the Revenue Runway framework so you can launch a profitable service-based business that meets a market need and generates income for you and your family.

By the time you finish reading this book, my goal is that you have 100% clarity on what you offer so you can start attracting the right kind of clients—people who need what you're offering and are happy to pay for your services.

No matter what happens with the economy (or who the current president is), you'll never have to worry when you have an irresistible offer that clients want and can get it into the hands of those who need it. I can't wait to show you how to get started!

Chapter 2
It's Time to Rescue Yourself

I admit it. I had unrealistic fairytale expectations when I started my first business. I think that happens to a lot of people, especially if you ease into having your own business like I did.

I've always known that I wanted to start a business; I grew up in an entrepreneurial family. My parents had a cleaning business, and although I wasn't interested in that kind of manual labor, I started brainstorming ideas for a business while I was still deployed to Iraq in 2008. When I returned to the States, I put my business ideas on the back burner. After a little time off, I went back to active duty as the head of public affairs for the Army Reserve for 22 states west of the Mississippi.

While my parents' cleaning business taught me about small business marketing, managing public affairs for the Army taught me the ins and outs of communications for large organizations and corporations. That background came in really handy when I found out I was pregnant in October 2009. As I mentioned earlier, I knew that being on active duty with a newborn was not what I wanted. I wanted to be there for my baby, and sending her off to daycare every day just felt wrong for me.

My job was intense, which didn't allow me to devote the time and attention my new baby needed. It was time to get serious about starting my own business, and I did. For the next six months, I started a little side hustle. I began building websites for friends and coworkers for $500 to $1,500 each during my off hours. (I know, I know. I was WAY undercharging, but I was just getting my feet wet and having fun doing it.) I wasn't ready to leave the Army, but I knew that day was coming. I wanted to prove to myself that I could do it.

In April 2010, I filed an LLC (Limited Liability Company) and, to my surprise, my little side hustle took off. By the time my daughter was just a few months old, I had enough clients to leave my Army job. I launched a business serving military business owners who needed help with their marketing. By 2013, I was traveling to military entrepreneurship events to market my business. Things were going great and in my mind, I had it made. What could go wrong?

As it turns out, a lot. Just as things were going really great with my business, I became a single mom of a young child in the middle of a messy divorce. Simply navigating life became difficult. It's not easy to balance a business with a young child while you're dealing with legal battles too. It started affecting my business, and it felt like things were falling down all around me.

I remember ghosting clients because I had to drop everything when my ex didn't show to pick up our daughter. I missed project deadlines, and I felt so overwhelmed that I quit following up with leads. I started losing clients, and then the worst happened: My lead flow dried up practically overnight. (I didn't know it at the time, but later discovered that my name was being dragged through the mud behind my back.)

The referrals I'd been receiving from the military industry came to a screeching halt. I didn't even know what was going on and my confidence took a huge hit. Although I realize I could have handled things better and my first business could have survived, I just needed to regroup and start over. The hard truth was I wasn't being the leader my business needed. My business wasn't set up to operate well when things went sideways.

I needed to do something different to get clients or I wasn't going to be able to pay my rent, put food on the table, keep the lights on, or pay my expensive legal bills. For the first time ever, I had to ask myself some hard questions about my business.

My most important question: What was the fastest, most sustainable way to take care of my daughter without having to leave her to get a job?

It took time for me to understand the real problem with my business: I didn't have the systems and processes I needed to generate my own leads and clients. I had to face the fact that a business couldn't rely on referrals forever. It was time for me to build a grown-up business. It was also time for me to face the fact that no one was coming to save me. It was time for me to save myself.

I grew my first business to six figures within two years, which was a great achievement. But it failed because I put all my eggs in one basket by working with only one type of client. When I left the military industry, I left behind all the connections and referrals I'd built. I was left scrambling for leads and clients. I vowed never to put my daughter or myself in such a vulnerable position again.

When everything fell apart, I had to focus on the important things first: my offer, my target audience, and my sales process. I was on my way to building a Revenue Runway that helped me stay on track and provided a direct path to sales even though my life was absolutely insane.

What the Revenue Runway Did for Me

The Revenue Runway Blueprint helped me reach six figures for my second business in half the time it took for my first business. But that's just the tip of the iceberg when it comes to how it helps me run my business every day.

First, it streamlined my offers and made my services easier to market and sell, which saved me time and helped my marketing budget. Then, I focused on revenue-generating activities within my business instead of all the shiny objects that didn't lead to any real growth.

Once I had my offers and sales processes figured out, I moved on to the day-to-day operations of being a service provider. I became serious about implementing internal systems and processes to assist with client onboarding and project delivery. I created clear and simple procedures that served clients well.

With my offers, sales, and internal operations under control, I was able to attract, land, and serve clients—even though my personal life was falling apart around me.

What Do You Do When It All Falls Apart?

If hard questions are staring you in the face right now, I want you to know I've been there and you're not alone. In fact, you're the reason I wrote this book. If you know in your heart that you want—no NEED—to take action now to start or grow your business, this book will help you answer the hard questions such as:

- Am I crazy to think about leaving a steady nine-to-five job I've invested years into?
- How do I generate leads and clients when I don't have a huge network?
- What if the business I have just isn't working?
- How do I put myself out there and break through the noise on social media?
- What if creating my own business doesn't work? What if I invest and it fails?

And maybe like me, the big question on your mind is: What's the fastest and most sustainable way to feed my family without having to give all my time to someone else's business?

When everything falls apart, it's hard to know how to pick up the pieces and turn them into a business. It's easy to get sidetracked by the strategies you see in YouTube videos and Facebook ads. But the truth is, a person can invest time and energy into busy work that doesn't produce results in terms of clients and revenue. You want to avoid falling into that at all costs.

Don't be afraid to ask yourself the hard questions. In fact, let me help. I'm going to break down some of those questions for you in the next chapter so you can identify any potential problems on the horizon as you start or grow your business.

No one is coming to save you. In this book, I'll show you how to save yourself using the Revenue Runway.

Reality Check

Early in my journey as an entrepreneur, I connected with someone I consider a mentor who is a former Navy SEAL and business owner. He told a story that was an absolute jaw dropper. In his early days as an entrepreneur, he worked with a contractor to renovate his leased office building. The owner of the building found out he was a Navy SEAL and offered to invest more than a million dollars to help him with his new business.

Great story, right?

I hate to break it to you, but chances are no one is going to walk through your door and hand you a million-dollar check. Would it be nice? Sure! But that's not the reality for most people.

If you want to change your life, you're going to have to rescue yourself. But before I go any further, let me get really clear about who this book is for so you have no doubt in your mind that it's for you.

Who This Book Is for

This book is for you if you're not happy with where you are in your nine-to-five job, military service, or corporate career. Maybe you don't love what you do. Maybe it doesn't fulfill you. Maybe you can't imagine keeping at it until retirement. Maybe you've reached as far up the ladder as you're going to get. Maybe you are one of the thousands who were recently let go in 2025 and it's left you feeling paralyzed.

You're ready to transition out, but you're not sure how.

This book is also for you if you feel like you're just trading your time for money working for someone else. You're sacrificing all your time to grow someone else's business. You can't take it anymore. You love the income, but it's coming at the expense of your time. Your goal is more freedom, and you know that having your own business can provide it to you.

I also wrote this book for you if you're experiencing circumstances in your life that make it necessary to start a business. You may have underlying reasons for wanting your own business such as having young kids at home, caring for an elderly parent, or dealing with a health condition that makes a traditional work setting difficult.

Whatever the reason, you know it's time to make a pivot and you're nervous. You don't expect people to suddenly beat down your door to work with you overnight, but you do want to know how to transition from side hustle income to replacing your nine-to-five income without losing your shirt. You need help, and you don't want to do it alone.

If you can relate to any of that: congratulations! You're in the right place to learn exactly how to make the pivot and start or grow your business. The Revenue Runway will help you get there without needing to achieve celebrity influencer status online, build a huge social following, or spend every spare moment creating video content.

Now It's Your Turn

I shared my story to give you confidence in your ability to start and grow your business. With the help of the Revenue Runway, you'll be able to make the most progress in the least amount of time without wasting money or getting stuck in strategies that don't work. It truly is the clearest, shortest path to success.

But it's up to you to take the first step.

Don't wait until you're forced to take action. It is easier to start now with the time you have than wait until you're in a desperate situation. You may think that you have plenty of time, but no one knows what's around the next corner. According to statistics, 59% of Americans are just one paycheck away from homelessness.[1]

---

1 Cynthia Griffith. "59% of Americans are Just One Paycheck Away from Homelessness." invisiblePeople, June 14, 2021, https://invisiblepeople.tv/59-of-americans-are-just-one-paycheck-away-from-homelessness/.

I was one of those 59%. I was constantly struggling to make my rent and car payment, and at one point, we were close to living in my car. My daughter didn't deserve that, and I had to figure out what to do for her.

When you have your own business, YOU are much more in control of your earning potential. You can better protect yourself and your family from financial vulnerability.

Here's something else to consider: Your desire to have something of your own won't disappear simply because you didn't take action. It will keep eating away at you.

It's my hope that by teaching you the Revenue Runway, you will stop putting off your dreams of starting or growing your business and take action NOW. I can't wait to show you how.

Chapter 3
Let's Be Real

As you read through the first few chapters of this book, I hope you feel both excitement and certainty about starting or growing your own business. You should be excited because owning your own business can absolutely give you the freedom to do what you love, while also providing you with more control over your time and income.

However, I'd be surprised if you weren't a little hesitant. Maybe you notice it when everything is dark and quiet in the wee hours; all the doubts and fears you've pushed to the back of your mind seem to come out to play.

- What am I thinking? I can't afford to quit my job!
- When am I going to find time to start a business on the side?
- What would I offer as services?
- Would anyone hire somebody with a brand new business?
- What if I can't figure it out?
- What if I fail?

If any of that sounds familiar, congratulations: You're a normal entrepreneur! You're not the only one who has ever wanted to start or grow a business with these same doubts and fears.

The root of the doubts and fears you have about starting or growing a business stems from being in a position where you have little to no perceived control over your time, money, or life. The answer to all of these questions is to take control. Instead of pretending these roadblocks don't exist, let's address them head on with the Revenue Runway framework so you can plow right through them.

My goal in this chapter is to put all those doubts and fears to rest. There are six common roadblocks entrepreneurs face when teetering on the edge of taking the next step in their lives and businesses. Read through each roadblock, then take a quick self-assessment at the end of each roadblock to learn which ones might be tripping you up the most.

Roadblock #1: Self-doubt

"I don't have a business degree or experience with starting anything like this. What do I know about starting a business?"

I completely understand where you're coming from. I didn't go to business school either. But here's what I've learned through my own experience and from working with others: Having a degree isn't a requirement for success. What matters more is your willingness to learn, adapt, and keep going, even when things get tough.

When I first started out, I struggled with comparison. My marketing packages included branding, websites, and logos.

My clients were happy, but I couldn't help but look around at the sleek, high-tech branding of major brands and corporations and feel like I would never measure up.

It took some time to build my confidence, but over the years, I've realized that I have a specific style that appeals to the right clients for me. When you're a service professional, you are part of the reason people want to work with you, it's not just your education or experience. If you're willing to listen to your clients and serve them well, that's what's most important.

Many people who have done amazing work just have a natural ability and are willing to step out and take action. But starting or growing a business is more about grit and determination than having the "perfect" credentials. Some of the most successful business owners I know didn't have any formal business education when they started. You know what they did have? The drive to figure things out as they went along.

There are so many resources available today (coaches, online courses, and membership programs) that make it easier than ever to learn what you need as you go. You don't have to know everything upfront. You just need to take that first step and trust that you'll learn along the way.

Self-Assessment: Is self-doubt your roadblock?
Rank yourself for the following statements. Answer each question honestly using the following scale:

1 = Strongly Disagree
2 = Disagree
3 = Neutral

4 = Agree
5 = Strongly Agree

Beliefs About Yourself

I often question my abilities, even when I have experience or success in a particular area._____

I feel like I am not as competent as others perceive me to be._____

When I achieve something, I tend to attribute it to luck rather than my skills or effort._____

I fear that others will discover I'm not as capable as they think I am._____

I avoid taking on new challenges because I doubt my ability to succeed._____

Decision Making and Taking Action

I procrastinate or overanalyze decisions because I'm afraid of making the wrong choice._____

I often seek reassurance from others before making a decision._____

I hold myself back from pursuing opportunities because I don't feel "ready" or "good enough."_____

I struggle with perfectionism and fear that my work will never be "good enough."_____

I compare myself to others and feel like I don't measure up._____

Handling Criticism and Setbacks

When I receive constructive criticism, I take it as proof that I am not good enough.____

A single failure or rejection makes me question my overall worth or ability.____

I dwell on my mistakes longer than I should instead of learning from them and moving on.____

I hesitate to share my ideas because I worry they might not be well received.____

I assume that others are more talented, capable, or deserving than I am.____

Scoring and Interpretation

15–30: Self-doubt is not a major obstacle for you. You may have occasional insecurities, but they don't hold you back significantly.

31–45: Self-doubt is present in some areas of your life and may be limiting your growth in certain ways.

1. Identify and Challenge Negative Thoughts
   When self-doubt creeps in, ask yourself: "Is this thought based on facts or fear?" Reframe the thought. Instead of "I'm not good enough," say, "I am learning and improving every day." Keep a success journal where you write down daily wins, no matter how small.

2. Take Small Risks and Track Progress
   Push yourself out of your comfort zone in small ways (e.g., speak up in a meeting or apply for a new opportunity).

Track moments when you take action despite fear. Over time, this builds confidence.

3. Reduce Comparison
Limit your time on social media if you tend to compare yourself to others. Remind yourself that everyone has struggles, even if they don't show them.

46–60: Self-doubt is likely a significant roadblock in your life, preventing you from pursuing opportunities or realizing your full potential.

Your self-doubt is preventing you from fully stepping into your potential. You might avoid opportunities, fear failure excessively, or struggle with imposter syndrome.

1. Strengthen Your Self-Identity
Make a list of past achievements and revisit it when self-doubt arises. Ask three to five people you trust what they consider your greatest strengths. This can provide perspective beyond your own doubts.

2. Take Imperfect Action
Instead of waiting until you "feel ready," commit to taking action despite self-doubt. Adopt a "done is better than perfect" mindset to break the cycle of overthinking.

3. Reframe Failure as Feedback
View setbacks as learning opportunities rather than proof of inadequacy. Ask: "What can this teach me?" instead of "What does this say about me?"

4. Limit External Validation
   Reduce excessive reassurance from others. Instead, develop self-trust by making small daily decisions independently.
5. Consider Mentorship or Professional Support
   Working with a coach, therapist, or mentor can challenge deep-seated self-doubt. Surround yourself with people who encourage and challenge you rather than those who reinforce your fears.

Roadblock #2: Lack of Support

"My partner/parents/friends think I'm crazy to want to leave a 'sure thing' at my nine-to-five job to start a business."

It's hard when the people closest to you don't understand your dream of owning a business. Your family, friends, or partner may not understand what you want. They may even try to discourage you. Mostly, they're just concerned because they care.

Although it is frustrating and disappointing, it's okay to let your loved ones off the hook. They're entitled to their opinion, but you don't need to rely on them as your business advisors. Tune out the negativity and stay focused on your goals. You're the one with the vision, and it's up to you to make it happen, even if others don't fully understand or support it.

The only opinion that matters is YOURS. You have to care about your future more than anyone else. You need people around you who understand your desire to own a business and who will help and encourage you. Let your loved ones be who they are in your life (your husband, sister, parent), and find your own network for support with other entrepreneurs.

Resilience has been key for me. I have had moments when I faced doubts from others. At times when my business was struggling, people would ask: "Why don't you just get a job? Why are you so insistent on owning a business?" That was hard, but I pushed forward.

One of the most important things you can do for yourself and your business, especially in the beginning, is connect with people who can support you. Find a mentor or advisor who can provide a proven plan or roadmap for what you need to do. Look for communities or memberships with people who are on the same journey. Talk to the people in your life who believe in you and your ability to make things work. Ask for their help and maintain your communication to help them understand why this is important to you.

It's not about proving naysayers wrong. It's about proving to yourself that you can do it. You'll make mistakes along the way, but that's part of the process. What matters most is that you keep moving forward. Once you get past the initial struggle, you'll experience breakthroughs and your confidence will grow.

Self-Assessment: Is lack of support your roadblock?

Rank yourself for the following statements. Answer each question honestly using the following scale:

1 = Strongly Disagree
2 = Disagree

3 = Neutral
4 = Agree
5 = Strongly Agree

Emotional and Personal Support

I feel like I lack encouragement from family and friends regarding my business idea.____

When I share my business goals, I often receive skepticism instead of support.____

I worry that starting a business will negatively impact my relationships.____

I struggle with self-doubt and could use a mentor or peer support system.____

I feel isolated and don't have anyone to talk to about my entrepreneurial challenges.____

Financial Support

I don't have personal savings or financial backing to get my business started.____

I'm unsure how to secure funding, such as loans, grants, or investors.____

I feel uncomfortable asking for financial help or investment.
____

I avoid starting my business because I fear financial instability.
____

I don't have a clear plan for managing my finances as an entrepreneur.____

Business Knowledge and Guidance

I don't know where to start when it comes to creating a business plan.____

I struggle to find reliable resources or mentors to guide me.____

I need help understanding legal, tax, or business structure requirements.____

I'm unsure how to market my business effectively.____

I lack role models or connections in my industry.____

Time and Energy

I feel overwhelmed balancing personal responsibilities with starting a business.____

I don't have a strong accountability system to keep me on track.____

I frequently procrastinate because I feel unsupported or unmotivated.____

I feel burnout or exhaustion just thinking about starting a business.____

I wish I had someone to help me stay focused and push through obstacles.____

Scoring and Interpretation

20–39: You have enough support to move forward. Your biggest challenge may be confidence or execution rather than external support.

40–59: You have some support but could benefit from more. Identify weak areas and seek specific guidance or encouragement.

60–79: Support gaps exist, but they're manageable. Consider strengthening your network and finding targeted help where needed.

80–100: Lack of support is a major roadblock. You may need to seek a mentor, a support group, or additional resources before moving forward.

Strengthening Emotional and Personal Support

Join us in the Revenue Runway Classroom. Our group is designed to help you succeed with free tools and done-for-you services. It's everything I wish I had when I started out on one platform!

- Find like-minded entrepreneurs: Join local or online business communities such as SCORE, Startup Grind, Indie Hackers, or Facebook Groups for entrepreneurs.
- Seek a mentor: Platforms like MicroMentor, SCORE, or LinkedIn can connect you with experienced business owners willing to guide you.
- Communicate with family and friends: If loved ones are skeptical, share your vision, explain why this matters to you, and set boundaries for unsupportive feedback.

- Find an accountability partner: Find a fellow entrepreneur or friend who will check in regularly on your progress and keep you motivated.
- Work in a collaborative space: Consider joining a coworking space or mastermind group where you can surround yourself with ambitious individuals.

Roadblock #3: Money

"I can't afford to quit my job and start my own business. I don't have the start-up capital."

Money is a roadblock that too often keeps people from starting a business. "I can't just quit my job. I've got bills to pay!" is something I hear a lot. And I get it, not everyone is positioned to launch a business and walk away from their career immediately. But that doesn't mean you can't start small.

It doesn't take as much money as you think to start a business. Most businesses that offer digital services can manage for a while with very low overhead. All you really need is a computer and a Wi-Fi connection to put yourself out there and start attracting clients. As your business grows, you can add more bells and whistles. I'll talk more about that in chapter 5. For now, just know that it doesn't take as much money as you think to get started.

No one said you had to leave your job right now. You can start a side hustle and build your business during your off hours. This provides you with the security of a regular paycheck while you establish your business. That's what I did while I was still on active duty. I worked my day job, then in my after hours, I built websites for people I knew in the military. It was definitely a balancing act for a while. I had many late nights and cups of coffee, but it was worth it. Within a few months, I had enough clients to retire from active duty and go all in with my own business.

You need to think about something else too. You might not want to quit your job because you need a steady paycheck, but there's no guarantee your job won't quit you. One day everything might be business as usual and the next you're walking out of the office with your box of stuff. Then where would you be?

Start working toward replacing your income now. People make room in their budgets for what they want. What are your priorities? Are there things you could sacrifice in order to start working toward your long-term goal of starting or growing your business now?

When my first business (a marketing agency for military entities) fell apart after my divorce, I had to pivot to serving industries outside the military. I knew I needed help. I was emotionally drained from my divorce and trying to do it all as a single mom, but I was committed to figuring it out. Life may have been kicking my butt, but I was far from ready to give up.

I had to redo my budget and find money for a coach. I was afraid my business would never recover. I settled on a coaching program that was $97 a month which was a real stretch for me. I had times when I didn't have enough money to pay the bills, but I had to prioritize my business growth because that would help me change my situation. It was one of the scariest but best decisions I've ever made because it gave me the direction and support I needed to grow faster.

The good news is you can get started right now with what you already have. Even if you're bootstrapping, the Revenue Runway framework works without costing an arm and a leg. In part 2 of this book, you'll receive my entire roadmap for starting or growing a business from the ground up, plus downloadable resources available inside a free, private online classroom. You are already holding the blueprint in your hands. All you have to do is keep reading!

Self-Assessment: Is money your roadblock?

Choose the response that best describes your current situation. At the end, tally your score to determine whether money is your true roadblock or if other factors are holding you back.

Business Planning and Strategy

Do you have a clearly defined business idea with a specific product or service?

    A. Yes, I have a detailed plan. (3 points)
    B. I have a rough idea, but it's not fully developed. (2 points)
    C. No, I'm not sure what my business would be. (1 point)

Have you researched your market, competitors, and customer demand?

    A. Yes, I have done thorough research. (3 points)
    B. I have some understanding, but I need more research. (2 points)

C. No, I haven't looked into it yet. (1 point)

Do you know the total startup costs for your business?

    A. Yes, I have a detailed budget and cost breakdown. (3 points)
    B. I have an estimate but need to refine it. (2 points)
    C. No, I have no idea how much I need. (1 point)

Resourcefulness and Alternatives

Have you explored alternative funding options (grants, loans, investors, crowdfunding, partnerships)?

    A. Yes, I have actively sought funding. (3 points)
    B. I know of options but haven't pursued them. (2 points)
    C. No, I haven't looked into other funding sources. (1 point)

Have you considered starting small or bootstrapping your business?

    A. Yes, I have a plan to start with minimal costs. (3 points)
    B. I have thought about it, but I don't know how. (2 points)
    C. No, I think I need a lot of money to start. (1 point)

Could you start your business as a side hustle while keeping your current income?

    A. Yes, I already have or am willing to start as a side hustle. (3 points)
    B. Maybe, but I haven't thought it through. (2 points)
    C. No, I think I need full-time commitment from day one. (1 point)

Mindset and Execution

What is your biggest reason for not starting your business yet?

- A. Lack of time or strategy, not money. (3 points)
- B. I feel overwhelmed and don't know where to start. (2 points)
- C. I truly cannot afford to take any risks financially. (1 point)

Have you taken any steps toward launching your business (even without money)?

- A. Yes, I have taken steps like building an audience, testing ideas, or learning new skills. (3 points)
- B. I've thought about it but haven't acted yet. (2 points)
- C. No, I feel stuck until I have enough money. (1 point)

Do you believe that creative problem solving can help you launch with little money?

- A. Yes, I am confident I can find a way. (3 points)
- B. Maybe, but I feel unsure how. (2 points)
- C. No, I believe money is the only way to start. (1 point)

Scoring and Interpretation

9–13: You believe money is the main obstacle, but is it really?

> You strongly feel that financial limitations are holding you back. However, many successful businesses start with little to no capital.
>
> Consider re-evaluating your approach. Can you start smaller, build an audience first, or find creative ways to test your idea?

14–20: You may need funding, but resourcefulness is key.

Lack of money is a challenge, but there are likely other factors (such as research, confidence, or execution) that are also holding you back.
Explore low-cost start-up strategies, partnerships, and alternative funding sources.

21–27: Money is NOT your biggest obstacle.

You are resourceful and capable of finding ways to start even with limited funds. Your main challenge may be planning, strategy, or execution rather than financial limitations.
Consider focusing on refining your approach and taking action now.

Roadblock #4: Time

"I'm still working my day job or getting my degree or a busy parent. I don't have time to build a business."

I know how hard it is to find the time to start or grow a business, especially when life is already full. I started my first business while I was pregnant and full-time active duty with the Army Reserves. I started my second business (esentially a rebrand) as a single mom with a small child during a messy divorce.

I didn't have much time, but I made the most of the small pockets I had and built my Revenue Runway business one brick at a time.

I spent every spare moment I could finding and serving clients. I attended local business events, veterans events, and church business events. I took advantage of every speaking opportunity that came my way. I found many clients by simply showing up and saying yes. As a single mom, it wasn't easy, but I made it work.

Whenever my daughter was napping, I worked on my business. Whenever a friend or family member offered to take her for a playdate, I took them up on it. Sometimes I even brought my daughter with me to events and meetings. I like to say that my daughter had probably been to more client meetings and networking events before age five than most adults attend in a lifetime. Thankfully, she was a calm and well-behaved baby.

The Revenue Runway is designed to help busy entrepreneurs build or grow their businesses in manageable steps that can be executed in short bursts of time. Many of you are reading this book right now because you have real-life challenges going on. These challenges make it necessary to build and grow your business now, and the Revenue Runway is what can make it doable, even amid chaos.

Steady action is what keeps momentum going and leads to real results over time. With this framework, you don't need to spend hours every day to make progress. The Revenue Runway is all about taking consistent, small actions, and it's laid out step by step.

Chapter 6 lays out a quick strategy you can use now to set yourself up for landing clients by clarifying your offer, identifying your ideal clients, and establishing online visibility. By focusing on client attraction while doing just one or two business building or growth tasks at a time, you'll build your bank account while you build your business brick by brick.

I've met people building businesses while working full-time, attending night school, or pursuing an MBA. It's hard, but if you're juggling chaos through no fault of your own, the Revenue Runway framework tells you exactly what to focus on, so there are no excuses for not taking action. You might think you don't have time but when you know exactly what to do, you will be astounded by what you can accomplish in 30 minutes a day. You CAN turn your roadblocks into a runway!

Self-Assessment: Is perceived lack of time your roadblock?
Rank yourself for the following statements. Answer each question honestly using the following scale:

1 = Strongly Disagree
2 = Disagree
3 = Neutral
4 = Agree
5 = Strongly Agree

Time Perception and Prioritization

You frequently feel like there aren't enough hours in the day to accomplish what you need. _____

You often say, "I don't have time," instead of exploring alternative ways to make time. _____

When you have free time, you struggle to decide what to focus on first. _____

You often start projects but fail to complete them due to time constraints. _____

Small, unexpected interruptions throw off your entire schedule. _____

Time Management and Productivity Habits

You lack a structured daily or weekly plan to manage your tasks. _____

You tend to multitask but still feel unproductive at the end of the day. _____

You avoid delegation because it feels faster or easier to do things yourself. _____

You frequently spend time on low-impact tasks while high-priority tasks get postponed. _____

You often underestimate how long tasks will take and you fall behind. _____

Mindset and Internal Barriers

You feel guilty when taking breaks and believe you should always be productive. _____

You often feel overwhelmed by your to-do list before you even begin. _____

You think others have more time than you, even when they have similar responsibilities. _____

You find yourself procrastinating and then blaming time constraints. _____

When you do have time, you struggle with motivation or focus.

———

Scoring and Interpretation

15–30: Time is likely not your biggest roadblock. You may have other productivity challenges, but a lack of time isn't the primary issue.

31–45: A perceived lack of time is impacting you, but some small adjustments in planning and mindset could make a big difference.

46–60: You strongly perceive time as a major limitation. Your biggest roadblock may not be time itself, but rather how you approach and manage it.

Guide to Overcoming a Perceived Lack of Time

If your self-assessment score suggests that a perceived lack of time is your roadblock, the good news is that time itself isn't the real issue, and instead your approach to it is! This guide will help you shift your mindset, improve time management, and boost productivity.

1. Shift your mindset: Reframe time as a resource. Replace "I don't have time" with "Making time for what will help me is a priority."
   This small shift forces you to acknowledge what truly matters. For example, instead of saying, "I don't have time to exercise," say, "Exercise isn't a priority right now." If that feels wrong, it's a signal to reevaluate your choices. Recognize that everyone has the same 24 hours. High

achievers don't have more time than you. They use their time more intentionally.

Time anxiety fuels inefficiency. Constantly stressing about time drains your energy. Instead of worrying, focus on making the best decision with the time you do have.

2. Prioritization: Stop managing time and start managing priorities.

Spend most of your time in the "Important but Not Urgent" category to prevent constant firefighting. Identify your "one thing." Each day ask: What's the one thing I can do today that will make everything else easier?

Batch similar tasks together. Instead of switching between tasks, group similar activities (emails, meetings, deep work) into time blocks.

3. Time management: Use strategies that provide structure to your day.

Use the 80/20 Rule (Pareto Principle): 20% of your tasks produce 80% of your results. Identify and focus on those high-impact activities.

Time Blocking (pre-schedule your focus time): Block out time for deep work, meetings, and breaks. Protect these blocks like important appointments.

Embrace Parkinson's Law: "Work Expands to Fill the Time Available." Set deadlines that force efficiency. If a task could take three hours, challenge yourself to complete it in 90 minutes.

Guide your decisions by the two-minute rule to eliminate micro-procrastination: If something takes less than two minutes, do it immediately. This prevents small tasks from piling up.

4. Mindset: Overcome internal barriers.
   Stop multitasking. Your brain can't do it effectively! Focus on one task at a time. Multitasking creates mental clutter and reduces efficiency.
   Delegate and automate. Ask yourself: Am I the only person who can do this task? If not, then delegate. Use automation tools for repetitive tasks (e.g., email filters, calendar scheduling, and AI assistants).
   Break large tasks into smaller steps. If you feel overwhelmed, break tasks into 5–15 minute actions. The momentum will help you finish.

5. Energy and focus: Optimize your productivity.
   Protect your peak productivity hours. Identify when you work best (morning, afternoon, evening) and schedule important work for those times.
   Use strategic breaks. Follow the Pomodoro Technique (25 minutes of work followed by a five minute break) to maintain focus.
   Prioritize sleep and recovery. Fatigue makes everything feel overwhelming. Well-rested minds work more efficiently.

Roadblock #5: The Economy

"It's a horrible time to start a new business because of the economy."

I won't sugarcoat it. We're living in crazy times. It seems like every other day there's a new headline about economic downturns, natural disasters, wars, and famines. You might be wondering why anyone would start a business right now with everything going on in the world. I say this is exactly why now is the time to take action and here's why: No matter what happens with the weather or the economy or the government, you still have the power to focus on your own growth. When it comes to making solid, proactive decisions for your future, one of the best things you can do is diversify. Don't rely on just one stream of income to get you through.

The worst number in business is one. If you're relying on one income stream, one job, or even one big client, you're putting all your eggs in one fragile basket. I once learned about a woman who worked her entire life on Wall Street. She put in long hours, never married or had kids, and faithfully invested in her 401(k)—only to lose $50,000 in a single day when the market crashed. I recommend having more than one income stream.

That's why it's so valuable to start building something that you control, own, and direct. The advantage of running your own business is that you get to decide who you serve, what you charge, and how you spend your time.

One thing I love most about my business is the freedom it gives me to be present for my daughter. I remember one morning that was particularly chaotic. My daughter almost missed the bus, and we were rushing to get her out the door. After getting her on her way, I took a moment to breathe then hopped on a Zoom call with a client.

It's those moments that make me grateful for the flexibility of my work. If I were still tied to a traditional job, those moments would be more stressful. I wouldn't have the same freedom to adjust my day around my daughter's needs. This business gives me the chance to balance being a mom and a professional.

At this point, you may be wondering why clients would want to hire you. As long as you have a skill set that solves a problem, you already have the foundation for a business idea. For example, a friend of mine has financial difficulties. She lives in a rundown home and wants things to change, but she's not sure how to turn her hopes into reality. She does have this one thing though—she loves to clean. I've been working with her to get a business idea developed using the same formula we've used with many others.

The Revenue Runway framework will help her learn how to take that business idea and turn it into a solid offer that resonates with people who need her services. And it can help you too.

You won't have to guess what will be effective in this economy. The framework helps you clarify and validate your offer, ensuring it will convert when it reaches the market. This process gives you more control and helps you move forward with confidence, even when things around you seem uncertain.

Self-Assessment: Is the economy or state of the world your roadblock?

Rank yourself for the following statements. Answer each question honestly using the following scale:

1 = Strongly Disagree
2 = Disagree
3 = Neutral
4 = Agree
5 = Strongly Agree

At the end, tally your score to assess whether external forces are causing your main roadblock or if internal adjustments can create a breakthrough.

Economic and Global Impact

The current economic climate has directly affected my business, job, or income opportunities. _____

Market trends in my industry have shifted in ways that make it harder to succeed. _____

Inflation, supply chain issues, or policy changes have significantly impacted my financial situation. _____

I have lost customers, clients, or job opportunities specifically due to economic downturns. _____

Global events (e.g., wars, pandemics, political instability) have caused setbacks I couldn't have anticipated. _____

Industry and Competitive Landscape

Competitors in my field are also struggling due to the same external conditions. _____

The demand for my product/service/job has decreased due to external market changes. _____

It feels like no matter how much effort I put in, outside conditions keep me from making progress. _____

There are fewer opportunities in my industry than before. _____

I have seen successful individuals or businesses in my field who seem unaffected by these challenges. _____

Internal Actions and Mindset

I actively seek new strategies and adapt when external factors change. _____

I have tested different pricing, marketing, or business models to counteract economic challenges. _____

I have invested time in networking, upskilling, or pivoting my career/business. _____

My mindset and habits play a bigger role in my success than external factors. _____

I can identify at least three things within my control that I haven't fully leveraged yet. _____

Scoring and Interpretation

45–60: Internal factors are your roadblocks. While external conditions may be challenging, your assessment suggests that personal actions, strategy shifts, and mindset adjustments can help you move forward.

30–44: You're dealing wih mixed factors. External conditions are influencing your progress, but internal adjustments (strategy, mindset, or approach) can still make a meaningful difference. It may be time to shift focus, explore new opportunities, or reframe your approach.

15–29: External factors are your roadblocks. The economy or global events are likely playing a major role in your roadblocks. However, identifying even small areas within your control can help you create a plan to navigate the challenges.

Roadblock #6: Fear of failure

"What if I try and fail? Why would anyone want to work with me?"

No one talks about how often people put business ownership on a pedestal, as if having your own business is the be-all and end-all of freedom and flexibility. But many small businesses are born out of necessity as a means to an end.

When life kicks you while you're already down, sometimes you have no choice but to pivot. I know people who started a business because they had a sick relative to care for at home. I know people who started a business because their military career was ending.

I started my current business in the middle of military service which transitioned into a messy divorce. It wasn't exactly what I'd planned for my life. But as everything around me started to feel chaotic and out of my control, I realized that building my own business was something I could own and shape for myself and my daughter.

I was also tired of being financially stretched. I wanted to be able to buy something simply because I wanted it without having to worry about my bank account. I was determined to create a life where I didn't have to rely on anyone else. I wanted to travel and send my daughter to good schools. The freedom to make my own decisions and set my own path gave me a sense of purpose at a time when I felt like so much was out of my control.

I had plenty of days when I felt like I was juggling too much: raising my daughter, dealing with legal issues, and trying to keep my head above water. But every client I took on and every project I completed reminded me of why I was working to create a professional opportunity for myself. The business wasn't just about money; it was about regaining control and building something stable for my family. Looking back, I can honestly say that starting my business during that rough season was one of the best decisions I have ever made.

When the pressure is on, it isn't always pretty, but that doesn't mean you should back down. It means you should keep going! If you're reading this book right now and think you couldn't possibly start or grow your business because everything around you is falling apart, you're wrong. You can, and the Revenue Runway framework can help. We'll go into more detail in part 2 of this book.

Just know that you won't be stuck in a trial-and-error process, hoping and praying that your offer is good and that your target market will want it. You'll know, and you'll have the tools and resources to help you make adjustments to your offer and your marketing as you go.

Will you experience failures and missteps? Yes, that's just life. Instead of viewing something as a failure, consider it a lesson and use those lessons to continue moving in the right direction. Fear of failure can prevent you from taking action, but don't let it.

Be careful how you measure yourself. Sometimes what we consider failure is us using someone else's standards. It doesn't make sense to compare yourself to a global brand or someone who has been in business for years. Measure yourself by your own progress.

I've faced my share of business challenges. I've experienced chaotic times in personal life that have forced me to rebuild. But every time I face a setback, I remind myself that setbacks are part of the journey. You don't need everything to be perfect. You just need to take one small step at a time. The Revenue Runway makes it simple and clear.

Self-Assessment: Is fear of failure your roadblock?

Rank yourself for the following statements. Answer each question honestly using the following scale:

1 = Strongly Disagree
2 = Disagree
3 = Neutral
4 = Agree
5 = Strongly Agree

Mindset and Emotions

I often hesitate to start new projects because I worry about failing. _____

The idea of making a mistake or being wrong makes me anxious. _____

When faced with a challenge, I immediately think of what could go wrong. _____

I feel like failure would reflect negatively on me as a person. _____

I tend to dwell on past failures rather than learning from them. _____

Decision Making and Risk Taking

I avoid taking risks, even when there's a chance of a great reward. _____

I overanalyze decisions to the point of inaction (analysis paralysis). _____

I often abandon ideas or projects because I fear they won't work out. _____

I let self-doubt prevent me from seizing opportunities. _____

I need excessive reassurance before making a decision. _____

Response to Failure

When I fail, I feel deeply embarrassed or ashamed. _____

I have a hard time moving forward after experiencing failure. _____

I compare my failures to other's successes, which makes me feel worse. _____

I try to hide my failures from others instead of sharing or learning from them. _____

I see failure as the end of the road, rather than as a learning opportunity. _____

Growth and Success Orientation

I struggle to celebrate my small wins because I worry they are not enough. _____

I hold myself to unrealistic or perfectionistic standards. _____

I procrastinate because I fear my work won't be good enough. _____

I hesitate to ask for help because I worry it makes me look weak or incapable. _____

I believe that if I can't do something perfectly, I shouldn't do it at all. _____

Scoring and Interpretation

20–39: Low fear of failure. Fear is not a major roadblock for you. You embrace challenges and setbacks as part of growth.

40–59: Moderate fear of failure. Fear sometimes holds you back but with effort, you can shift your mindset toward resilience.

60–79: Significant fear of failure. Fear is likely preventing you from taking necessary risks and moving forward. Consider mindset shifts, self-reflection, and support to overcome this challenge.

80–100: High fear of failure. Fear is a major roadblock in your life. It may be helpful to explore deeper strategies such as coaching, therapy, or structured personal development to break free from limiting beliefs.

Once you've moved the roadblocks out of the way, the path forward is clear for the next steps and that means taking action! Let's dive into chapter 4 where I'll break down why action is so important and where to start.

Chapter 4
The Key to It All

Starting a business isn't for the faint of heart. You'll have times when you deal with imposter syndrome and mindset traps that make you want to freeze. The good news is that there is a cure for analysis paralysis (and actually the key to it all): It's taking action!

Why action though and not mindset? Because according to a Journal of the Association for Psychological Science, taking action influences your thoughts which helps strengthen your mindset.[2] Sometimes we wait to take action until we "feel" like we are ready. We assume that if we feel uncertain or unqualified, it must be the truth so we stay stuck.

When you take action despite how you feel, your feelings align as your brain sees the results of your actions. You're doing yourself a favor by ditching the excuses, taking action, and allowing that action to strengthen your belief.

---

[2] Susan Goldin-Meadow and Sian L Beilock, "Action's Influence on Thought: The Case of Gesture," *Perspectives on Psychological Science: A Journal of the Association for Psychological Science* 5, no. 6 (2010): 664-74. https://doi.org/10.1177/1745691610388764.

And of course, I had to learn the hard way.

Action Is the Cure

When I first started my business, I was full of excitement and confident that no matter what happened, I could figure things out. Little did I know that my refusal to take action would almost be the death of my business! Back then, I was charging what I thought people would pay and tried to keep my prices low enough to attract clients quickly.

I charged $500 for a three-page website. I told myself it was the right price because it would attract business and build momentum. I was totally wrong. It didn't build momentum. It brought my business to a grinding halt. By not raising my rates, I kept myself trapped under an income ceiling of my own making, and I was totally tapped out in terms of time.

As weeks and months went by, the wheels began to come off. I was working so hard, juggling clients and projects, but the numbers just didn't add up. I wasn't making enough to cover everything, let alone justify the hours I was working. I had the clients and the workload, but I was still struggling financially. And I was exhausted. I'd go from one project to the next without taking a breather. It felt like no matter how much I scrambled, I was stuck in the same place. I was overworked and underpaid to the point where I couldn't even afford to hire help.

The reality of my situation finally hit me one day while I was talking to an industry friend. She looked at my prices and said,

"Why are you charging so little? You're putting in the work, and you deserve to be compensated for that."

That was a moment of clarity for me. I realized that by not taking action and raising my rates, I was trapped in a cycle of overworking and undervaluing myself.

I'd been waiting to raise my rates until I felt like I "deserved" it. I achieved results for clients, but I'd be able to get better results for clients if I charged more. I'd have more time because I'd be taking on fewer clients.

So, I took a deep breath and raised my rates. I was nervous and thought I'd lose clients or scare people off. But something amazing happened instead. My clients respected me more and recognized the value of what I offered. I began attracting clients who didn't just want the cheapest option—they wanted quality. Raising my rates gave me breathing room to grow both professionally and personally. It was the turning point I needed to build something sustainable and not just scraping by.

Looking back, I wish I'd raised my rates sooner, but I'm grateful for the lesson. Things were never going to change in my business if I didn't do something different. I had all the other pieces, but until I took action and raised my rates, I didn't have a foundation that would allow my business to thrive.

This book contains my entire blueprint on how to start and grow a business using my Revenue Runway framework. But here's the thing—it only works if you do. The best business blueprint in the world won't do you one bit of good unless you take action.

Ready, Set, GO!

In previous chapters, I showed you how starting or growing your own business is the key to taking control of your life and future. I hope that by now you recognize that this is for you and that you can do this. But it's one thing to think, "Oh, sure, yeah, I'm going to start a business!" and another to actually step into it.

Here are five common questions that prevent people from taking action. I want to put your mind at ease about the issues related to these questions. In the rest of this chapter, I will discuss these five questions and answer each one by explaining how the Revenue Runway framework can help.

Question #1: Where should I start?

Right now you're probably thinking "Okay, Kalen, it's easy for you to say that action is the key, but I don't even know what to do first!"

Boy, do I get that!

When I started building my business, I was all over the place. I didn't know where to begin or how to make my vision a reality. I found myself purchasing every low-ticket offer I came across on how to grow an online business. I'd heard plenty of advice about marketing and finding clients. The collection of ebooks, downloadable guides, and masterclasses cluttering up my hard drive was truly impressive.

Yet, I was still stuck. I felt like I was trying to piece together a hundred different strategies without any idea what the finished result should look like. I spent months collecting information and doing nothing with it until I discovered an approach that completely changed my life and business.

I studied business systems and spent thousands of dollars and hours learning everything I could about building and scaling businesses. During that time, I realized that there were certain core steps that all successful business owners implement. I combined what I learned from these experts to create a framework that cuts through the noise and provides a clear path to build an online service-based business.

The Revenue Runway framework is a proven blueprint for building or growing a business. It makes the step-by-step progression of creating your offer, identifying your audience, and taking targeted steps easier to understand and implement. It doesn't overload you with theory but guides you with actionable steps that move you forward quickly. Use what you learn about the Revenue Runway to set your focus and gain the confidence to take real action instead of just spinning your wheels.

Question #2: How many people do I need to hire to operate the Revenue Runway?

I have a really simple answer for that: zero.

Yep, that's right. You don't need to hire anyone to start your own business. You can start your business as a solopreneur freelancer. The Revenue Runway will help you get your one-person show off the ground and grow without wasting time or energy on things that will only slow you down.

But that doesn't mean you don't need anyone. Starting a business, even as a side job, is doable, but it does take work. It can be stressful and mentally draining. You need a support system of other entrepreneurs who understand what it's like to dream of having your own business and are aware of the challenges and pitfalls.

Early on in my business, I learned some hard lessons with clients that led to missed payments from clients and legal threats, which resulted in many sleepless nights worrying about whether I was protected. That's when I knew I needed the right legal support, so I reached out to an attorney friend who specializes in trademarks, copyrights, and contracts.

This friend didn't just help me protect my business. They gave me the confidence to guide my clients to protect theirs too. Now, I can ensure they have access to the resources they need to grow their businesses without the fear of being left vulnerable. I'll pass along some of that information to you later in this book when we talk about starting your business from scratch in chapter 9.

Another unexpected yet incredible partnership I experienced was with my husband, who is a mental health counselor. Many challenges in business are as much mental and emotional as they are strategic. His support helped me work through my own mental blocks and build resilience. That perspective now forms a significant part of the Revenue Runway. With his insights, I'm able to help clients tackle the personal challenges that come with business ownership.

These connections are much more than professional allies. They're the pillars that helped me create a business that's stronger and more grounded. This is a reminder that building a successful business isn't just about the work. It's about having a support system that helps you navigate and grow through every challenge.

I've mentored many freelancers. My business has even been their business wingman. We know the ins and outs of guiding people through the early stages of business development, but we can only help so many freelancers at a time. One of the reasons I wrote this book is to help more solopreneurs get off to a good start, then grow and scale knowing they're not alone.

I also urge you to surround yourself with other people like you. Facebook groups are great places to network with others. Don't be afraid to ask questions online and look for people you can learn from.

Question #3: How quickly can I make progress?

Everybody wants to know how long it will take to get their business off the ground, turn things around, or scale their business to the next level. It all comes down to one thing: action. How quickly you get results depends on how quickly you take action.

The good news is that you're already ahead of the game because this book is your literal action plan. There are three simple steps:

- Step 1: Read a chapter.
- Step 2: Fill out the self-assessments as you come across them.

- Step 3: Download and complete the Revenue Runway Blueprint Workbook from the book website. See the Resources section of this book for the link.

As you go through this book chapter by chapter, you'll learn how to identify whom you will serve, how to create a bulletproof offer, how to sell your services, and how to streamline your processes. We'll dive into specific action plans for people who are just starting a business, people who are struggling in business, and people who are ready to grow and scale their businesses. I can't wait to get started in the next part of the book!

Question #4: What else will I need to invest in to make this work?

The words "start a business" come with some preconceived notions about what "business" looks like. You might be envisioning an office space, a fancy tech stack, new computers and software, and a business wardrobe. But some of you are at the very beginning and thinking about offering freelance services to clients. If that's you, start with what you have and work your way up.

Use the free resources that are available to you. As you land clients and build your business, you can make decisions about how to allocate your business budget. It doesn't take as much as you think to bootstrap a business.

Some of you are reading this knowing that you've been planning this move for a while. Maybe you have a little startup nest egg, or you've been putting away a portion of your nine-to-five income to fund your dream. Later on, I'll break down what makes sense to spend on and what doesn't according to the Revenue Runway so you're allocating assets in a way that helps create sustainable growth quickly.

Before you take action, you need to consider where to invest your time, energy, and resources. There are many distractions that can divert your focus and in the next chapter, I'm going to tell you what they are and how to avoid taking action on the wrong things.

Chapter 5
The Problem With Action

Action alone isn't enough. I know I just finished telling you that action unlocks 80% of the results waiting for you when you use the Revenue Runway.

There's just one problem.

Not all action is created equal, especially when you're trying to start or grow a business, your life is falling apart, or you're still working at your day job. You don't have much time, and plenty of other things need your time and attention. You want to do what will get you the best results fast. Not every course of action will get you to where you want to go.

Many people focus on the wrong things when starting their own businesses. Don't get me wrong, it's not necessarily that these actions are bad. There are just a lot of things the flashy gurus telling you what you "need" to do when you're starting a business that don't always work.

In this chapter, I will pinpoint things people do that aren't helpful in the early stages of starting or growing a business.

You may have already done some of these, and if you have, that's okay. Don't feel bad. It's not your fault. You were doing your best with the information you had at the time.

I want to save you from spending more time, energy, or money on things that can be done later. That's why in the next chapter, I'll teach you the Revenue Runway framework step by step so you have an exact blueprint of the most impactful things to do that will allow you to start landing clients and generating income as soon as possible.

What if You're Doing It Wrong?

There's a mile-long list of actions that people are told to take when they want to start their own business. Just type "how to start a business" into a web browser and you'll see millions of search results pop up. It's overwhelming and intimidating. No wonder one in four small businesses fail within the first two years! Unfortunately, the numbers only climb as the years go by. According to the US Bureau of Labor Statistics, 48% of small businesses fail within five years, and 65% of those that remain will close their doors within ten years.[3] I don't want you to become a statistic. I want you to have a business that lasts for as long as you want it to.

When it comes to offering online services, the type of business I'm talking about in this book, much of what you'd need to start a traditional brick-and-mortar business isn't necessary, such

---

[3] Maggie Davis and Dan Shepard. "Percentage of Businesses That Fail–and How to Boost Chances of Success." lendingtree, February 7, 2025, https://www.lendingtree.com/business/small/failure-rate/.

flow. For now, you can search Fiverr for an affordable deal on a graphic designer or create one yourself using a free tool like Canva.

Creating a Detailed Business Plan

I previously thought you needed a detailed business plan to start a business. That's what everyone in the professional world said, but I no longer agree. You don't need a detailed business plan unless you're pursuing a large loan or external funding.

Is it bad to have a plan? Of course not. The problem with creating a complicated business plan is that people get stuck in "planning mode," drafting endless business plans and perfecting every detail, but they never get started. They feel productive, but they're not moving forward. If you wait to have every detail lined up, you'll miss out on opportunities. I know veterans who wanted to start a business, but they spent years planning and nothing ever happened.

In order to start your business, you only need to know who you want to serve and how you want to serve them. I will walk you through that step by step in part 2 of this book.

Following All the Free Advice

One big lesson I've learned is to be very cautious about taking free advice from people who've never built a business. Early on, I received all kinds of advice from well-meaning friends and family who had never actually run a business.

They meant well, but their advice wasn't grounded in experience. They would say things like, "You should put an ad in the newspaper" or "Why don't you just make some business cards" without any understanding of what it actually takes to start and grow a business.

What I've realized is that running a business is its own world, and you only truly understand by being in it. Free advice can sound nice (especially the free part), but if it comes from someone who hasn't been in the trenches making sales calls, marketing their services, and managing projects, it can lead you down the wrong path.

Now I stick to learning from people who have actually been where I want to go. People who have built something themselves but are further ahead than I am in the journey. Their advice is grounded in real challenges and successes, not ideas or theories. It's important to get input from those who truly understand the ups and downs of entrepreneurship.

With all that in mind, how do you right the ship?

I made all of the above mistakes when I started my first business. I saved up $25,000 while I was deployed. But instead of doing what I should have been doing (figuring out what services I wanted to offer and connecting with potential clients), I paid someone to build a website for me and design some fancy business cards. I made a Facebook business page and used my personal profile to promote it.

Do you want to know how many clients those actions helped me land? Zero. I was just throwing spaghetti at the wall, taking whatever random actions I'd heard someone on the internet recommend.

The only reason I landed any clients was because I called myself a military marketing agency. At the time, no one else had that niche so I stood out as the go-to person for military businesses. I wasn't being purposeful about the actions I took, nor was I seeking advice from people who were succeeding at doing what I wanted to do.

The good news for you is that you can do it better than I did. You can start with purposeful, proven action based on the Revenue Runway framework as I teach it to you in the next section of this book. We'll start by figuring out your offer FIRST so you can clearly describe the value and results you can bring to clients. Then I'll teach you how to get those first clients and test your marketing.

We'll take it step by step. You will learn from the data you gather as you go even if you're on a small budget. A formal plan can come later once you know more about what your clients need and what actually works to help them.

Congrats! You've made it through part 1 of this book! In part 2, we're going to dive into exactly what the Revenue Runway is and how you can use it to help create a business that will survive and thrive no matter what life throws at you.

Part 2

From Roadblocks to the Revenue Runway

Chapter 6
Clear the Way for Clients

Before we dive into the Revenue Runway, I want to highlight one thing that can seriously sabotage your success, and we need to clear it out of the way before you serve any clients. Even if you follow the rest of this book by the letter, failing to address the following issue will hold you back: victim mindset

Why a Victim Mindset Will Sabotage Your Business Growth

A victim mindset is where you constantly feel powerless, blame others for your circumstances, or wait for external rescue. Victim mindset directly undermines the three essential traits needed for a successful business: resilience, adaptability, and willingness to take full ownership of your outcomes.

At the core of entrepreneurship is the principle of ownership. When things go wrong, such as missed goals, lost clients, or failed launches, a growth-oriented leader asks, "What could I have done differently?" In contrast, someone with a victim mindset deflects with comments such as, "The market is too saturated," "Nobody supports me," or "This just isn't fair."

The victim mindset absolves the individual of responsibility. But without accountability, there can be no progress. If everything is someone else's fault, then change and success is out of your hands.

Running a business means constantly encountering problems. Customers complain. Ads flop. Systems break. A victim mindset interprets problems as proof of injustice or personal attacks which results in decision paralysis or emotional spirals.

A growth mindset views challenges as puzzles to be solved. The difference between the two mindsets isn't the presence of problems; it's whether you believe you can overcome them. Thinking like a victim puts your power outside of you. Entrepreneurial thinking, or thinking like a survivor who is in control, keeps your power within you.

Business growth requires energy: mental, emotional, and sometimes even spiritual stamina. A victim mentality drains your energy and prevents you from being productive because it fosters helplessness, cynicism, and emotional volatility.

A victim mindset also repels high collaborators needed for success. Employees, partners, and clients are drawn to confident, empowered leaders. If your internal narrative is one of being constantly wronged or unlucky, you'll inadvertently attract others who validate or mirror that dysfunction such as people who expect handouts, stir up drama, or are full of excuses.

When you view the world through a victim mindset, it is like wearing blinders. You're so focused on what's not working that you miss what could work. You might overlook a niche market, a potential client, or a way to pivot simply because your mental bandwidth is consumed by resentment or self-pity, both of which are natural outcomes of having a victim mindset.

Opportunity is often disguised as hard work, feedback, or failure. If you view these as personal attacks instead of stepping stones, you'll miss the very doors that could lead to your breakthrough.

Business growth is about momentum: take action, get feedback, adjust, and then act again. A victim mindset short-circuits this loop by inserting emotional friction at every turn. Each setback becomes a reason to stop rather than a reason to evolve.

What's worse is that the victim mindset waits for ideal conditions (more support, a better economy, less competition) before motivating you to move forward. But there are no perfect conditions. Growth comes to those who take imperfect action repeatedly.

If you're trying to grow a business, the most dangerous story you can tell yourself is: "This is happening *to* me."

The most powerful story? "This is happening *for* me."

You are not powerless. You are not stuck. You are not defined by what didn't work yesterday. You are defined by what you choose to do next, and building your Revenue Runway is the perfect next step!

Chapter 7.0

Introduction to the 3 Pillars of the Revenue Runway

Welcome to the 3 Pillars of the Revenue Runway, my step-by-step process for starting and growing a business when you are navigating tough times. Starting your own business requires planning and preparation. Because you have this book, you have a proven plan at your fingertips.

I can recognize a brand-new business owner on social media from a mile away. They are very excited about starting their business and assume that finding clients will be easy. "I'm going to tell everybody what I'm doing, and everyone will want to work with me!" They post consistently for a while but around six months in, they quiet down and you don't hear as much from them. Sometimes that's because their business launch went really well, and they're too busy to post. Other times, it's the opposite. Their business didn't survive, so they got a job because running their own business was much harder than they thought it would be.

I had my daughter not long after I launched my business. When you have kids, life seems to intensify. Then I went through a messy divorce, and suddenly I was dealing with trying to balance client meetings with childcare. I burned a lot of bridges with clients during my divorce because of the juggling I had to do. My life was a mess. My clients didn't know what was going on behind the scenes, and I didn't want to share any details about my personal life with them because that felt unprofessional.

I remember one instance when my daughter unexpectedly needed someone to pick her up. I was on my way to a meeting at a coffee shop with a new client, and I had to cancel so that I could pick up my daughter. I know I must have seemed flaky to the person I was supposed to meet, but I had no choice. Sometimes the client was kind and understanding, and we'd reschedule and continue to work together. Other times things didn't work out. Every day I told myself, "If I lose a client, it's no big deal. I'll just find a new prospect." And I did because I had built my Revenue Runway, just like you will learn in part 3.

Reaching your destination is going to require planning and expertise. Just like flying an airplane, building a business isn't something you can accomplish with just the push of a button. Without a flight plan, a navigation system, and fuel, you'll never get off the ground. You need a plan that helps you put all the pieces into place.

Introduction to the 3 Pillars of the Revenue Runway

Your Revenue Runway is that plan. When your life goes sideways, your Revenue Runway will be a saving grace because you won't have to wonder what steps to take. Like every good pilot on a mission, you'll have:

- A plane (your offer)
- Fuel (your target audience)
- A navigation system and flight plan (your services and sales strategies)

In the rest of this chapter, I'm going to break down the three pillars of the Revenue Runway:

Chapter 7.1: Irresistible Offer. You'll learn what an irresistible offer is and what components contribute to one that sets it apart from what your competition offers.

Chapter 7.2: Ideal Client Avatar. You'll learn how to determine who to serve and what their needs and pain points (problems and challenges) are.

Chapter 7.3: Solid Sales Strategies. You'll learn how to communicate with your target market about your offer that helps you generate leads and book calls.

I used these three pillars when I started my first business, and you can use them to build your business too. The Revenue Runway sounds simple, right? It is, yet many business owners fail to figure those three pillars out before attempting to get clients. I don't want you to struggle to get your business off the ground, so let's start at the very beginning by talking about Pillar 1: an irresistible offer.

Chapter 7.1
Irresistible Offer

What first comes to mind when you think about a successful business? A nice logo? A sharp-looking website? A lot of employees? Those things are all great, but they are not the key to a successful business. A business succeeds when it offers a product or service that people want that solves a problem they have. This solution should create a desirable result. Each business needs to clearly and effectively communicate the problem and the solution to the right people: buyers. In other words, a business succeeds when it has a compelling offer. And a business will function even better if its offer is irresistible.

An offer isn't simply a service or a product. It's a solution to a problem your ideal client is actively looking to solve. An irresistible offer packages your skills, your experience, and your value into something that feels like a no-brainer to the right person. Having a good offer is the first step to attracting and landing clients, but you also need to ensure it suits your lifestyle, your time, and your skill set. In chapter 8, I'm going to ask you to brainstorm and record your answers to two questions:

- What talents and skillsets do I possess?
- How can I turn those skills into a service or product?

For now, let me give you examples to help you understand what working through this process looks like. I've filled out a chart for a fictional man we'll call Bob Jackson. Bob has a background in accounting. He wants to start his own business so he can be more available to care for his wife who has just been diagnosed with early onset Alzheimer's disease. Here's what Bob's initial brainstorm might look like:

Bob the Accountant	
What talents and skill sets do I possess? *I love helping people get clarity on their financial situations.* *I love helping set budgets and manage cash flows.* *I love investing in the stock market.* *I love helping people make good decisions about their money.* *I have an accounting degree and have worked as a corporate accountant for 20 years.* *I have a healthy portfolio of investments and have helped my friends and family members invest too.* *I'm really good at balancing books.*	How can I turn those skills into a service or product? *I could offer services for:* *Financial planning* *Accounting* *Bookkeeping* *Retirement planning*

You can see that Bob definitely has marketable skills that he would enjoy using to provide solutions to people who need his help. He could start a business as a financial planner, bookkeeper, or investment coach, and make money doing something he's good at and enjoys.

For our next example, let's say it's about a 34-year-old public relations specialist we'll call Maggie Abrams who has been unhappy in her corporate job. Now that her kids are older and in school, she's tired of telling them she can't attend their school activities because she's at work. She'd love to start her own business so she can be more flexible with her schedule while still contributing to the family's income. Let's take a look at what Maggie's list would include.

Maggie the Public Relations Specialist	
What talents and skill sets do I possess?	How can I turn those skills into a service or product?
I'm good at making and editing videos of my kids.	*I could offer services for:*
I'm creative and enjoy learning new software	*Video editing for social media content*
I've grown my social media accounts for my mom blog	*Social media management*
I can identify social media trends and leverage them for growth	*Advertising and marketing services*
I know exactly what types of videos to create to gain followers and expand my reach	*Content creation for businesses and entrepreneurs*

Maggie has marketable skills too. With her video editing talent and knowledge of social media trends, she could offer services as a content editor, video strategist, or social media manager for businesses that know content is a way to grow but don't have the time to do it themselves.

The Gold Is in the Details

Identifying what services you could offer is only the first step. When you think about your offer, the gold really is in the details. Your offer is your way of saying, "Here's what I've got that can help you, and here's what you get if you say yes." Your offer is the entire package you present to your customer or client which includes:

- What you're selling (a product, service, or both)
- What the thing you're selling does for the client or customer (the benefit or result)
- What it costs
- Any other extras that are included (like bonuses, guarantees, or special deals)

For example, if you were selling lemonade your offer might be: "Get a cold, fresh-squeezed lemonade for $2. Comes with a free cookie. Today only!"

The offer isn't just lemonade. It's the experience of cold, delicious citrus and sugar on your tongue on a hot day, the price, the cookie, and the incentive to buy.

You need to ensure that what you're offering will sell, meaning your opinion isn't the only one that matters. You must factor in what people in the market want. For example, you may really enjoy dog grooming, but if you live in an area where dogs aren't allowed, it could be hard to find clients. That's why the next step is to look at the market to see what's selling. You'll need to do some market research.

Why Market Research?
Are the services or products you've come up with already being offered? Are they selling well? You can find out by doing market research. From what I've seen in the business world, market research is wildly underrated but absolutely critical. This section is about helping you understand why market research matters and what you'll use it for. I'll walk you through how to do it in chapter 8.

Market research is vital because it helps you dial in on where people are spending their money. Market research can make the difference between building an offer you hope will sell and building one based on research about what the market wants. The good news about doing market research is that it doesn't require you to have a fancy degree or a big audience. You just need to be willing to ask questions and listen to the answers.

Get curious about what people are struggling with, what they've already tried that didn't work, and what they're actually willing to pay. Without that information, you're just guessing. If you get your offer wrong, trying to make sales or land clients can quickly get frustrating and expensive. When you've done your market research, you can create an offer that speaks clearly to your dream clients, and they start to wonder if you're reading their minds.

Most people skimp on market research, so when you do even a little, you're instantly ahead of the game. You don't need a research team or an expensive survey platform. You just need to know where to look. Some of the best places to gather insights are completely free and already at your fingertips.

Start with platforms people already use to search for solutions like Google and YouTube. Tools like www.AnswerThePublic.com can show you what questions people are actually asking in real time. These tools help you find the phrases and pain points that your ideal clients are already thinking about, so you can create an offer that meets them exactly where they are right now. (I'll walk you through how to use a few of these tools for market research in chapter 8, and we'll get clear on who your ideal clients are in chapter 9, so don't worry about figuring it out on your own.)

Now, let's start putting your services and your market research together to build an irresistible offer.

What Makes an Offer Irresistible?

First, we need to cover one of the finer points of your offer that can either make or break it. If you've ever felt stuck trying to figure out what to offer (or worse, like you're offering something but no one seems to want it), it's usually because the offer is built around what you do, not what your ideal clients need.

An irresistible offer doesn't lead with your services. It leads with a result that solves a problem for a specific type of person. What are they dealing with right now that's costing them time, energy, money, or peace of mind? What would they pay to stop dealing with it? Focusing on that is what will make your offer irresistible. We'll talk about how to identify that person (your ideal client avatar) in the next section. For now, here are some examples of what I mean about focusing on the result.

- If you're a graphic designer, you're not just selling logos. You're selling brand clarity, credibility, and the confidence that comes from having a business that looks as legit online as it actually is in real life.
- If you're a virtual assistant, you're not just selling inbox management. You're selling peace of mind and time back to your clients.
- If you're a web developer, you're not just selling websites. You're selling a platform that brings in leads and sales while your client sleeps.
- If you're a copywriter, you're not just selling text. You're selling words that move people to buy the products and services of your clients.

Before you worry about naming your package or pricing your offer, ask yourself which specific problem you want to solve and which kind of transformation it creates. An irresistible offer clearly answers:

- Who is this for?
- What problem does it solve?
- What result does solving that problem deliver?

Once you've nailed down the transformation your offer delivers, the next question is: How do you stand out in a crowded market full of competitors offering similar products and services? Even if you're offering something valuable, it won't matter unless people can see why they should choose you over the others who solve that problem too. Let's take a look at how to do that.

Helping Your Offer Stand Out

I'll never forget a prospect who said on a call, "There are tons of marketing agencies out there. Why should I hire you?"

I answered, "Because I'll answer the phone when you call me."

He laughed, and that's when I knew my business was going to be okay. Even though I was facing competition from larger, more established marketing agencies, I stood out.

Competing with established businesses that are larger and fancier can be a real concern for new business owners. Don't worry, small businesses can compete with big ones if they position themselves differently. Even in industries like cleaning and restoration, where big players like Servpro dominate, smaller businesses can stand out by offering personalized service and displaying a greater attention to detail.

Some of the best success stories start from the tiniest beginnings. Years ago, I ran a local farmers market in Arizona. I met so many incredible small business owners! One was a family that had turned their living room into a bakery stand. In Arizona, you're allowed to sell baked goods from home, and they went for it. You'd walk into their house, and boom! A bakery. And they didn't just do a bakery in their home; they took it on the road and did pop-up bakeries all over the area.

When they embraced their identity as a pop-up bakery, people loved joining them on the journey. The owners shared pictures of their pies on Instagram and partnered with local businesses that agreed to sell their treats. We bought some mini pies for our coworking space, and people loved them.

This specific bakery started out taking special orders and hosting pop-up shops. Then they adapted their pastries to each venue and enjoyed their traveling content. Within a few years, they opened a full bakery with a storefront. It was amazing to see them grow so fast. Their stuff was just that good. I wouldn't be surprised if they had multiple locations.

That story reminds me of a mother and daughter duo making macarons. I learned quickly that it's "macaron," not "macaroon" (which is a different type of cookie). The daughter joined and started experimenting with flavors like Fruity Pebbles which sounds wild but is fantastic. They started small by baking for local events and generating word of mouth.

One day, an event planner for the luxury brand Chanel attended an event where they served their cookies. She approached them and said, "We're doing a red carpet pop-up event, and we want your macarons there." This event wasn't even local. It was in New York City.

I loved that the mom was her daughter's biggest cheerleader. And not just at home, but everywhere as she helped with the business marketing. The mother would say, "My daughter's an amazing baker. These macarons are hard to make, but she's mastered it." And she wasn't wrong. Those cookies were delicate and perfect every time. That Chanel gig was a turning point for them. As a result, they ended up on TV and their business took off. Their upward growth all started because they kept putting themselves out there.

That's what I love about entrepreneurs like them. This mother and daughter team didn't wait for everything to be perfect or for someone to hand them success. They started small, kept improving, and remained consistent. Even when they were working full time or juggling other responsibilities, they kept going. And eventually, something caught fire.

They specialized in unique flavors and branded them for client events. It wasn't about selling. It was about solving a problem (what do I serve guests at my event that will make a real statement?) and creating something that people wanted. An irresistible offer should contain something that people can't get anywhere else. It could be your guarantee, the way you provide services, your unique qualifications, or your customer service. Now that you've seen this amazing macaron example, how can you learn to communicate about the special solution you offer to clients? Time to find out.

Communicating Your Offer

Once you have a general idea of the types of products or services you want to offer and what makes your offer unique, it's time to start thinking about the basics you'll need to start talking to people about it. Every offer needs a good name and clear pricing. If you want assistance coming up with a name, setting your prices, or creating an offer description, visit your Revenue Runway classroom where I've provided some ChatGPT prompts that can help.

Offer Name

Choose a unique name for your offer that connects it to your brand in a way that's memorable and intriguing. Here are some examples using fictional offer and brand names:

Type of Brand	Brand Name	Offer Name	Why It Works
Coaching or consulting brand	The Clarity Collective	The Clarity Catalyst	Plays off the brand name while promising a clear transformation
Copywriting Brand	Bold Type Co.	The Bold Launch Blueprint	Uses the word "bold" for the brand name to reinforce a distinct style or tone
Fitness Brand	StrongHer Studio	The StrongHer Reset	Feels like an exclusive program under the StrongHer umbrella—identity and empowerment are baked in
Mindset Brand	Inner Shift Method	Shift Sessions	Feels directly connected to the brand promise—transformation from the inside out
Mentor Brand	The Launch Lounge	Lounge to Launch VIP Day	Keeps the cozy, insider vibe while pointing toward results

Offer Price

You can charge hourly, flat fee, or do a combination. Not sure which pricing model you should use? Here are my recommendations:

Charge hourly if the scope of work and time required vary depending on the client. When you charge a flat fee without knowing how much time it will take, you risk getting underpaid, especially if you have a client who likes to make extra requests outside the scope of work you've previously agreed upon.

Charge a flat fee if you know exactly how long the offer will take to fulfill. Not having to track your time can be really nice. When you know exactly what to expect from a project, it's also easy to help the client understand what to expect.

You can also use a hybrid pricing model where you charge a retainer fee for a specific amount of work or time and then charge hourly for additional time or services. This works great when you don't know exactly what will be needed at the beginning of a project, yet it ensures you'll be covered for your time and efforts.

Additionally, you can play with how you split up payments. For example, this year my agency launched a new package geared toward a specific audience. I initially set the price point at $10,000. Although the package is well worth the price because it delivers big results for clients, it was a hard sell. I needed to get creative with my pricing structure to get the yes. I ended up creating two options. The first option was $10,000 which included a speedier delivery of services. Package number two was $6,000 paid in three installments of $2,000 per month, and it was delivered over a longer period of time. The second option was much easier for new prospects to say yes to, and it was a win for everyone.

Whichever pricing model you choose, choose a price point you feel confident about that's also an easy yes for the client. Make sure you research the rates of well-established businesses that offer similar services to compare prices. You can raise your rates as you book out your services, get results for clients and customers, and gather testimonials and reviews. One of the most important parts of selling is believing that you can help the people who hire you. Confidence matters.

In the beginning, you need to prioritize closing sales with confidence. This means doing the work in the background to make sure you have the right mindset, as I discussed in chapter 6. Confidence is contagious, and if you're confident in how you sell your services, your prospective clients will also feel confident that you can deliver the promised results.

Once you've created your irresistible offer (the kind that makes your ideal clients feel like you read their minds), the next step is narrowing down exactly who those ideal clients are. You don't want to waste your energy marketing to just anyone. Your offer becomes exponentially more powerful when it's paired with a crystal-clear understanding of who it's for. So next up, we're focusing on your Ideal Client Avatar.

Chapter 7.2
Ideal Client Avatar

When my first business failed after my divorce, I went through a tough time professionally. I had been really good at serving military business owners, and it hadn't been difficult for me to attract clients. After all, there weren't many other service providers who were military professionals serving military business owners.

But when it was time to start over and branch out, I had to completely reinvent my business. I had to go back to square one and figure out my clients again. One of the first things I did was create a brand-new ideal client avatar (a detailed profile that described my ideal client) for my brand-new business.

Knowing your ideal client avatar helps determine how you communicate with them in many ways: what your core message about your offer is, where you advertise, and which social media platforms you use. The clearer you are about your ideal client, the better marketing results you will achieve.

There are nearly infinite potential niches to choose from, which can be both a blessing and a curse. It's a blessing because when it's your business, you get to pick. It's a curse because trying to figure out how to narrow it down on your own can be overwhelming. That's just extra stress you don't need right now. I'm going to make it as simple and easy as possible to identify your ideal clients and customers in this chapter. Then I'll walk you through how to create your own Ideal Client Avatar step by step in chapter 9.

Finding the Audience for My New Offer

Once I decided what I wanted to offer in my digital marketing agency (lead generation services), I focused on my ideal client. Lead generation services are in high demand. After all, every business needs leads. The problem was that there were (and still are) tons of agencies out there that already offer lead generation services. I needed to narrow my focus so I could stand out. Plus, I didn't want to serve everyone.

I started brainstorming the following questions:

- Which types of businesses struggle with lead generation? This indicates a problem that they would pay to solve.
- Are there certain types of businesses I've worked with before and achieved results?

Then it hit me: There was a perfect client right under my nose! Growing up, my dad owned a restoration cleaning company. I knew this type of business inside and out. Did these businesses need leads? Yes! Could I solve that problem? Also yes!

Restoration cleaning companies offer need-based, time-sensitive services. The problem is that these restoration company owners have no way of knowing who is searching for their services, which leaves them in the dark when it comes to seeking out potential customers. If someone's house is flooding right now, the homeowner is looking for immediate help. The restoration company that appears first in their feed or search engine will be the one they call.

These restoration companies are not lead generation experts, but I am. I know how to use software to identify who's searching for restoration services and immediately target them with an ad for a restoration company within their local service area. As far as I know, there isn't another agency that offers a service that works in real time like mine, which makes my agency a perfect fit for restoration cleaning companies.

Now that my offer and audience match, it is much easier for me to target the right clients and communicate what I can do for them.

Dial in on Your Who

One of the best ways to help your offer stand out is to get specific about the real person you're marketing to. Consider the virtual assistant services offer we've been referring to. Let's say the competition markets to business owners in general. Yes, that means there will be a larger number of prospects, but it's also quite broad. What if you niched down to only certain types of businesses such women-owned or those in specific geographic areas? You could focus your marketing in a way that businesses targeting a broader audience couldn't without potentially alienating a segment of their audience.

Let's say you love photography and want to become a professional photographer. That's pretty general, right? It doesn't really stand out or grab the attention of a specific type of person. But when you're clear about your exact ideal client, it changes the way you communicate. For example, maybe you love babies and want to offer newborn photo sessions. That means you'll want to target pregnant women. You should look for places online and in person where pregnant women gather. Instead of just saying "I'll take your pictures" to anyone in general, you can say "I'll help you capture those first precious moments with your new family member."

Let's say you want to offer search engine optimization (SEO) services. You might be tempted to think, "Well everyone with a website needs that, so I should just market to everyone." That may be true, but blanket marketing (marketing to a very general audience) is often less effective than targeted marketing. What if you decided to narrow your focus to insurance agencies? You could focus on their specific problems and challenges. You'd know exactly who to reach out to and how to communicate with them. Instead of promoting general SEO services, you can position yourself as the right expert at the top of their search results.

But not everyone will be an ideal client for you. Let's talk about how to identify red flags so you can avoid the stress of working with clients who aren't a good fit.

Red Flags

Identifying your ideal clients and customers helps with more than clarity on whom to market to. Getting clear on who you want to serve can help you spot red flags so you can avoid nightmare client experiences.

Every business owner I've ever met has had a nightmare client experience. That's the last thing you need if life is already challenging you. I'm not saying you'll be able to avoid difficult clients, but there are red flags. Here are three common nightmare client types and the red flags that will help you steer clear of them.

Nightmare Client #1: They don't want to pay your rates.

Not everyone will be able to afford your services, and that's okay. That specifically isn't a red flag. It just means that the client is not a good fit for you. The difference is between someone who can't afford your rates and someone who doesn't want to pay your rates. Not wanting to pay your rates indicates that they don't value your services.

When a client doesn't value your services, they will always focus on price instead of the results delivered. You want clients who are excited to work with you and happy to pay. They have a clear understanding of the value you bring to the table, which will lead to a better experience for everyone involved.

Red Flag Indicators:

If you're on a sales call with a prospective client and you hear comments like the ones below, proceed with caution because they might be a future nightmare client.

- They tell you so-and-so can do it for less.
- They ask if you can do it for less.
- They talk negatively about how expensive other service providers are.

Nightmare Client #2: They're impossible to reach.

This client constantly misses calls, is late giving you the information you need, or is always unavailable. No matter what your offer is, this type of nightmare client makes it difficult to deliver results because they aren't committed to following through on what you're helping them with. You'll likely spend a lot of time and energy trying to track them down.

My agency learned to be aware of this with restoration company owners. They are busy, spend a lot of time on job sites, and aren't always available when it's most convenient for us. When we onboard clients, we clearly communicate expectations upfront so they know what we need.

A good client will make time to meet with you and work collaboratively to get the best results possible.

Red Flag Indicators:

If you're on a sales call with a prospective client and you hear comments like the ones below, proceed with caution because they might be a future nightmare client.

- They talk about their day-to-day lifestyle as if they never have a moment to spare.
- They don't seem to be available for calls during normal working hours.

- They don't want to play a part in giving you the information you need so that you can do your job.

Nightmare Client #3: They don't respect your boundaries.

Boundaries? What boundaries? This client calls at all hours day or night and expects you to provide extras at no charge. They treat you like an employee instead of a fellow business owner, which is not a fun experience.

A friend of mine used to create sales catalogs for cattle auctions. She enjoyed the work, but there was one particular client who was difficult. This client expected her to pick up the phone every time they called—even if it was in the middle of the night, on weekends, or during holidays. They were a nightmare client and when she finally let them go, she couldn't believe how long she'd put up with that less-than-ideal situation.

A good client will respect your boundaries and treat you like an equal and partner to achieve a specific goal.

Red Flag Indicators:

If you're on a sales call with a prospective client and you hear comments like this, proceed with caution because they might be a future nightmare client.

- They ask if you'll be available on short notice if they need something.
- They say they expect you to be available at the drop of a hat.
- They speak dismissively about their employees or other service providers.

Putting It All Together

You might be new to identifying your ideal clients or customers, and that's okay. Like I said in chapter 7.1, we're brainstorming and not setting things in stone. If you haven't produced a result for someone yet with the service or product you'd like to provide, look for someone you can offer your services to for free. This is a great way to get some experience and testimonials for your work. To help you brainstorm your ideal clients and customers, head to chapter 9 where I explain how to create your own ideal client avatar.

Refreshing your ideal client avatar can be helpful even if you've been serving clients or customers for a while. Maybe you're reading this book to leverage the Revenue Runway framework to grow and scale your existing business. Trends, the economy, and culture change over time, so by refreshing your ideal client avatar, you'll likely identify helpful new insights that will create ways for you to get better results with your marketing.

Once you are clear on the clients you want (and don't want) to serve, you're ready to turn your attention to Pillar 3: Solid Sales Strategies. In the next section, I will share some simple sales strategies that will help you start advertising your services. I'm also going to give you tips on creating your offer description and mastering the art of following up.

Chapter 7.3
Solid Sales Strategies

One of my favorite sales calls was with a small business owner from San Diego. He ran a local business and had been handling his own marketing from day one. He'd hired a web developer and a branding expert to create a basic online presence, but beyond that, it was all him. He wrote emails, ran ads, sent postcards, and worked hard to grow his business without an in-house team.

When we spoke, I knew immediately that he was my ideal client. He came prepared and already knew exactly what he wanted. This made our consultation less like a traditional sales call and more like an interview or conversation; I didn't have to convince him or overcome any objections. After ensuring my offer aligned with his needs, he was ready to move forward. My ads and website communicated what he needed to know in order for him to want to work with me before we actually talked.

I was impressed by how well he understood the value of a good marketing agency. He'd been in the trenches himself, so he knew how much time and energy it took to make marketing work. He also understood the cost of wasted time and money from past efforts. He wasn't worried about pricing or skeptical about our process. He was maxed out. He'd hit his own limitations and recognized that he needed to bring in help so he could take his business to the next level.

That call was a dream scenario for me. I was communicating with someone who knew enough about marketing to ask the right questions, understood the value of what I brought to the table, and had a clear vision for where they wanted to go. It wasn't about selling him on my service. It was about partnering with someone who was ready to trust the process and invest in their business's growth. It was a match made in sales heaven!

Once you've created your irresistible offer and identified your ideal client avatar, you're ready to start making sales. That's all you need to focus on right now: offer, audience, and sales. In this section of the Revenue Runway framework, I will provide you with some simple sales strategies that you can begin using to present your offers in front of the right audience. It is my goal for you to start having conversations with ideal clients about your offer so that you can build your business despite challenges in your personal life.

I've broken everything down into step-by-step processes to keep everything simple. When you're building a business designed to support your life, you don't need complicated strategies that require expensive tools or software. Maybe you're working around challenges like health issues or a divorce. Maybe you just want the freedom to work where and when you want so that you have more time to spend with your family. No matter what brought you here, my simple and proven approach to sales can help you land clients and build your income. Let's dive into the first item: creating your offer description.

Creating Your Offer Description

You'll need a simple statement to communicate who and how to serve. This will also act as a description of what your offer is and the results that your offer will deliver for the client or customer. You'll want a clear and straightforward sentence that you can discuss with anyone.

When you create your core sales message, you'll want to clarify several items. Inside your Revenue Runway Blueprint, you'll find Core Sales Message worksheets to complete. These worksheets will draw from your Irresistible Offer worksheets and Ideal Client Avatar worksheets. As a reminder, you can find each worksheet in your Revenue Runway private classroom (which you can access via the link in the Resources section of this book).

In chapter 10, I'll walk you through your Core Sales Message worksheets and provide practical examples of core message statements based on our fictional business owners, Bob and Maggie. But for now, let's focus on your Core Sales Message. You'll want to be ready with three pieces of information as you get started:

- WHO you serve
- WHAT they want
- HOW you serve them

Your core sales message will give you a quick and clear answer to provide when someone asks, "So what do you do?" Your core sales message can be used for more than just quick elevator pitches too. You can use it on your website, on your social media business page description, and on any printed materials you create in the future. Let's look at the results of this process in more detail.

Sales Call Secrets

Once you create your core sales message in chapter 10, you'll be able to clearly communicate who and how you help. It's a great conversation starter with members of your target audience and can lead to sales calls. In the beginning, sales calls will likely be your main avenue for landing clients. I know that can sound intimidating, but let me take the "ick" factor out of the idea of sales calls right now by framing them differently for you.

Remember the call with the prospective client from San Diego that was more like a conversation than a pitch? That's how you should think about these conversations as well. A sales call is just another conversation that provides you with an opportunity to connect with someone, understand their challenges, and see if your offer aligns with their needs. If your offer is a good match, then the sales call is less about selling and more about helping them solve a problem conversationally. That takes a lot of the pressure off.

For me, this type of call is never about following a strict sales script. Prospective clients appreciate it when you're genuine and present during your conversations. They want to know that you care about their business goals. By the time the San Diego business owner reached out to me, he was exhausted and ready to let someone else take over his marketing. I remember his call so clearly because he wasn't there to be sold to. He already knew what he wanted and said, "I've taken this as far as I can, and now I need someone who knows what they're doing to take it further." He wasn't worried about pricing or trying to haggle. He simply wanted results and was ready to trust the process I had outlined in my marketing materials.

Calls like his remind me why I do what I do. It's not about pitching or convincing clients; sales is about finding people who already see the value in what I offer and showing them how I can help.

I think people feel like they have to be some kind of sales guru to land clients on calls, but you don't. That can actually backfire depending on who you're talking to. Imagine if I had taken a very pushy sales approach during the call with the San Diego business owner. He would have felt like I wasn't listening to him, which could have discouraged him from working with me.

The hard sell never works on me either. I had a sales guy tell me once, "Yeah, my style of sales is like…" and then named a well-known marketer who has always seemed pretty salesy to me. I couldn't help but think, "That doesn't seem like a good thing to me." I don't love pushy, high-pressure sales calls and needless to say, I didn't buy whatever he was selling.

Many buyers are accustomed to hopping on multiple sales calls with different companies before they make a final decision. Many times, they make that decision based on how the sales call and follow-up actions go. As we work on refining your sales technique and avoiding the pushy calls most potential buyers dislike, let's talk about how to prepare and perform well on a call.

Prepping for the Call

If it helps, think of the sales call as a first date. How do you prepare for that first interaction? You put effort into how you look and present yourself. You consider some questions you'd like to ask. You make a plan for where you want to go and what you'd want to do. Why would you put so much effort into a first meeting? Because that first date determines whether you get a second date.

Let's apply this concept to sales calls. How do you prepare for a sales call? Your approach during the call needs to match the person you want to work with. Once you've identified your ideal client, take a step back and consider their point of view. They have a problem you can solve, but they don't know you're the solution yet. Before they decide to work with you, they want to know:

- Do you really understand my problem?
- Can your offer solve my problem?
- Why will this approach work for me when others haven't?
- Can I trust you?
- How are you different from other service providers who have let me down before?
- How much does it cost?
- Is it worth spending the money instead of just doing it myself?

- What will happen if I don't solve this problem?
- What will happen if I do solve this problem?

These are great points to consider as you prepare for that first call. If you enter the call already knowing the answers to those questions, you'll be prepared to have a good conversation about how you—specifically—can solve their problem. But, this will only work if you show up feeling confident that you can deliver what you promise.

Show Up with Confidence

One of the biggest challenges I see people face when they first start making sales calls is a lack of confidence. If you don't feel confident about your offer, that doubt will show during the call. I'll be the first to admit I've struggled with this in the past.

I remember when my agency launched a new service. I was really nervous because I didn't have any case studies from my own business yet, even though I had results using the same techniques in the business I had previously worked for. Sure enough, on one of the first sales calls I made for this new service, the person on the other end asked for a case study. Instantly, my brain froze. I hoped they couldn't hear my heart pounding.

When you're doing something new and don't have your own results or testimonials, it can be a tough spot to be in, and it can negatively affect your confidence. There are two strategies you can use to handle the "too new for case studies" stage: a paid strategy and a free strategy. We're going to look at each option.

The Paid Strategy

The first time someone asked me for a case study before I had one, I almost panicked until I remembered that I had a backup. I had joined a certification program to learn this specific skill, and I was working with partners to sell the service. I kept myself together long enough to say, "Let me look into that for you." I went straight to the partners, and they provided me with case studies and brainstormed responses to sales objections. With their help, I was able to return to the client on a second call where I closed the deal.

When you're new or offering something new, you can partner with someone you know who already has case studies, such as a coach or mentor. Pay to learn from them and ask questions about how to handle sales objections. I've invested in certifications where I learned a skill and then had permission to use the case studies from that organization or coach. But what if you're looking for a strategy that's less spendy? I've got you covered.

The Free Strategy

The second option won't cost you anything but time, and it's a great way to build case studies. Find someone who's your ideal target audience and ask if you can do some free work for them in exchange for a case study or testimonial. For example, let's say you're a website designer for dental clinics. You could call local dentists and ask if you can build them a website for free. In return, you ask that they be honest and provide you with feedback that you can use for a case study or testimonial. They wouldn't even have to use the website if they didn't want to.

As you make more calls and serve more people, your confidence will grow. Landing your first few clients in the early stages is just the beginning. Keep going! As we move to the next concern, this is a concept that can make or break even the calls where you offer free services.

Listen and Care

Another challenge I see people face is coming across as uncaring. Sometimes this is just because they're nervous. They don't want to say the wrong thing, so they don't engage well with the prospective client.

If you feel that nerves could be a challenge for you, remember that a sales call is just a conversation. The person on the other end of the line is simply someone who has a problem you can solve. Don't be afraid to be yourself. If they ask a question you don't know the answer to, that's okay. It's 100% acceptable to say, "I don't know the answer to that right now, but let me do some digging and I'll get right back to you." People appreciate honesty. Often, they can tell if you're just grasping at straws or guessing answers.

When you truly take the time to listen and care about what your prospective clients need, you learn valuable information that will make your offer stronger and your sales calls more successful.

When my agency launched a new offer to restoration cleaning companies, we quickly generated over 100 booked calls. These business owners had a real need, and they were looking for a solution. I couldn't wait to start landing clients!

This was a new target audience for me, and I was sure I had the right offer for them. Turns out, I was wrong. As I made call after call and received no after no, I started listening closely and asked questions to discover what they really wanted and needed. I learned that they already had 90% of the services I included in my offer.

I swear, I botched two-thirds of the calls before we finally focused on the one thing they really needed: intent-based search leads. Once I was clear on the details, the last third of the calls went great! Was it fun getting all those rejections? Heck no! But the information I gathered from conversations helped me create the exact offer they really needed so I could start knocking sales calls out of the park.

In the next chapter, you'll be researching your competitors and clarifying your ideal target audience before discussing sales. Why do you think I'm having you do that? Because when you do that work on the front end, your offer will be clearer and more attractive from the start. As you get people on sales calls, talk to them. Don't be afraid to ask them questions such as:

- What are you already doing for XYZ?
- How is that working for you?
- How much are you paying for it?

The information you receive is invaluable and will help your future sales calls go better.

Let's move on to the final, and maybe the most important, piece of the sales process: your follow up.

Following Up

One of the biggest mistakes you could make with the sales process is failing to follow up. It's easy to think that follow up is no big deal and doesn't matter. But follow up is where most sales occur. Not everyone is ready to sign on the dotted line the minute a sales call is over, but that doesn't mean they'll never be ready. Be willing to provide value and help them out as a matter of principle, regardless of whether they hire you or not. When you follow up, you'll be the person who's still on their radar when the time is right.

People need time to think, especially if they are going to invest their hard-earned money and trust someone else to solve their problem. When you follow up, you give them the opportunity to learn more about your offer and to build trust and connection with you as a person. Here are some of my favorite ways to follow up:

- Create a value-packed freebie or guide that shows them what you do and what working with you will look like.
- Make a personalized video recap of the call thanking them for their time and email it to them.
- Send a follow-up email. Better yet, add them to a follow-up sequence of emails. My agency has a 27-piece email sequence that sends emails to prospective clients every other week for an entire year. You don't have to go that big right away, but it's food for thought.
- Mail a thank you card along with a business card or a small desk calendar featuring your logo—something to keep your name and brand in front of them. People love to get real mail, and it's rare these days!

In his book, *Sell It Like Serhant: How to Sell More, Earn More, and Become the Ultimate Sales Machine*,[4] real estate agent Ryan Serhant discusses the lengths he goes to when it comes to following up with clients. He shares a story about wanting to be the agent for a large apartment complex that was going to be for sale soon. At the time, he'd never worked on a deal that big, and he wasn't a well-known agent. The owner dismissed him at their first meeting. But instead of taking that as a no, Serhant decided to follow up in a very clever way.

He purchased a bookshelf and had it shipped to the property owner. A week later, he sent him a book. The week after that, he sent another book. He sent a book every week for the next two years! The property owner called and said, "Fine. You can be the agent for my property. Just stop sending the books!"

I'm not suggesting you go that big. This was a multi-million dollar real estate deal. Unless you're a Manhattan real estate agent, that kind of follow up isn't practical. But you can do something, right? As they say, the fortune is in the follow up, so follow up regularly after each of your sales calls. And since we've covered the last step of the Revenue Runway framework, it's time to start taking action.

Now Let's Build Your Revenue Runway!

We've covered a lot of ground in part 2 with the Revenue Runway framework. You learned the three pillars of the framework, and now you're ready to build your own Revenue Runway with me! Congratulations!

---

[4] Ryan Serhant, Sell It Like Serhand: How to Sell More, Earn More, and Become the Ultimate Sales Machine. Legacy Lit, 2019.

Part 3 will walk you through building each of the three pillars we covered in chapter 7. You'll create your irresistible offer in chapter 8, then work your way to chapter 9 to build your ideal client avatar. You'll finish this process by creating your core sales message in chapter 10.

Part 3

The Blueprints to Your Revenue Runway

In part 3, you will be building your own Revenue Runway Blueprint. Visit your Revenue Runway classroom to download the Revenue Runway Blueprint Workbook. Inside the workbook, you'll find fillable worksheets where you can create and record your Irresistible Offer, Ideal Client Avatar, and Core Sales Message. When you've finished all three, you'll have completed your Revenue Runway Blueprint, and your business will be ready for takeoff!

Chapter 8

Your Irresistible Offer Worksheet

In this chapter, you're going to build your irresistible offer based on your unique skills and talents. I'll show you how to research as you go to ensure you're meeting a need in the market and providing a result that people are willing to pay for.

Step 1: Determine Your Talents and Skillsets

Remember the two questions I said you should ask yourself at the beginning of chapter 7.1? It's time! Start by writing as many answers as you can to the question: What talents and skill sets do I possess? Record your answers in the first column of the table in the "Your Talents and Skillsets" section. You can find the workbook linked in the Resources section of this book.

Brainstorm all kinds of ideas and you can narrow things down later as you go. Knowing this information about yourself and the market can help you focus on viable services that you could offer clients (ones that won't burn you out or keep you working for pennies). When you're done with the first column, move on to the question in the second column: What product or service could I offer based on those skills?

When you know which services you'll provide, you'll be able to create a strong, irresistible offer. Plus, you'll know that you genuinely enjoy doing the business you're creating. You want your offer to be competitive in the marketplace too. The next step, market research, will help you discover your competition, what they're offering, how they communicate about it online, and what they charge.

Step 2: Market Research

Research Your Competitors

Do a keyword search for the services you want to offer using your favorite search engine (I like Google). Let's say you think you'd like to offer virtual assistant services. You'd type in "virtual assistant services" or "virtual assistant services near me." The search engine will display the top search results for those keywords. These will be sites you'll do market research on. Copy and paste the URLs of the first few listings into the "Market Research" section of your Irresistible Offer worksheet.

View Competitor Websites and Social Media Accounts

Now that you've identified your competitors, take a close look at their websites. You can find a lot of good information about your competitors' offers online, and this information will help you create your own offer. Look for information on the following and add it to the "Market Research" section of your Irresistible Offer worksheet:

- What services the business offers. Be specific about the words and language they use to describe their services.
- How much they charge. Include information for both single services and packages.
- What are these businesses doing that you like? It can be helpful to visit their social media accounts for a behind-the-scenes look at the day-to-day operations of the business.
- Does what you see fit with your lifestyle?

Want our help with market research on your competitors? Head to the Resources section of this book where you'll find a link to book a call.

Build Your Irresistible Offer

As you can see from your competitor and market research, a strong offer includes more than just the services you provide. You need to consider how you package your services, what you call that package, and what the price will be. Next, take a step back and review the information you've collected about your competitors while keeping your own services in mind.

Now dive into the "My Irresistible Offer" section of your workbook. Fill in the spaces with information about your own offer. When you've finished, congratulations! You've brainstormed an offer you can build your business around, and this is just the beginning. We go deeper into pricing, delivery, and more in my Revenue Runway program.

In the next chapter, I'll walk you through how to identify the people you'll market to. Then, you'll create your ideal client avatar profile to help you reach the right people with your future marketing.

Chapter 9

Your Ideal Client Avatar

Ready to create your own ideal client avatar? Turn to the Ideal Client Avatar section inside your Revenue Runway Blueprint Workbook found in your private Revenue Runway classroom. Follow the worksheets step by step and gather information about your ideal clients and customers as you go. When you're done, you'll know where to market your offer and how to reach your ideal customer.

Step 1: Cover the Basics

First, fill in your answers to the following questions in the table provided in your workbook. I've filled in the examples below with information about our fictional characters Bob Jackson and Maggie Abrams, as well as their ideal client avatars. We'll start with Bob. After considering his talents, skills, and the activities he enjoys, Bob decided to launch a business doing financial and retirement planning.

Bob Jackson's Example:

What type of people need the solution to the problem my offer solves?	Are there certain types of people I've worked with before and gotten results for?
1. Pre-retirees and retirees (ages 50–70) • They're nearing or entering retirement and need clarity on whether they've saved enough. • They're concerned about how long their money will last and how to withdraw it wisely. • They may have scattered accounts, pensions, or investments and need help creating a unified strategy. 2. Middle-aged professionals (ages 35–55) • They're earning decent incomes but are unsure how to build long-term wealth. • They need help with budgeting, managing cash flow, and investing strategically. • Many are behind on retirement planning and want to "catch up." 3. Caregivers or those with major life transitions • People who are navigating caring for a spouse or aging parent and need financial clarity to make good decisions.	I've spent years helping my own parents and siblings navigate these exact questions by creating personalized retirement plans, budgeting for fixed incomes, and investing for long-term security. I've seen firsthand how much peace of mind it brings when someone has a clear, step-by-step plan. That's the kind of support I want to offer to others who are in the same boat: people who want to retire with confidence, avoid costly mistakes, and make smart, informed decisions about their money.

- They may need to scale back their work and want to ensure their finances are secure while managing caregiving costs.

4. DIY investors who need a second opinion
- These individuals have been managing their money independently but now want expert guidance to optimize or validate their strategy.
- They may be nervous about market shifts, taxes, or missing out on something big.

5. People who feel overwhelmed by money decisions
- They're not necessarily broke—but they don't feel in control.
- They're looking for someone who can explain things clearly, without judgment, and help them feel confident about their financial future.

Now that you know what this part of the process looks like for Bob, let's look at our second example. Maggie decides to offer social media management services to business owners. Here's what her ideal client avatar basics might look like.

Maggie Abram's Example:

What type of business owners need the solution to the problem my offer solves?	Are there certain types of businesses or people I've worked with before and gotten results for?
1. Coaches & Consultants • Life coaches, business coaches, mindset coaches, health coaches • These entrepreneurs are the brand, and they need to be consistently visible to attract clients.	Not yet.
2. Online Service Providers • Virtual assistants, copywriters, graphic designers, course creators • These folks are great at their own zones of genius but often struggle to stay consistent on social media.	If not, who could I help for free to get experience and testimonials?
3. Brick-and-Mortar Small Business Owners • Boutique owners, salon owners, local photographers, fitness studio owners • They need engaging, local content that draws people into their space or brand, but don't always have the time or tech knowledge to execute.	
4. Etsy Shop Owners and Creatives • Makers, crafters, artists, and digital product sellers	

• They want to grow their presence on Instagram, TikTok, or Pinterest but need help turning their work into scroll-stopping visuals. 5. Realtors and Real Estate Professionals • Realtors need local visibility and personal branding—but don't want to spend hours editing videos or guessing what to post. 6. Influencer Moms or Aspiring Content Creators • Women like Maggie—mompreneurs who are growing blogs, affiliate income, or brand deals—who would relate to my vibe and benefit from my editing and trend expertise.	My friend Sam who has an Etsy shop My chiropractor My stylist

Step 2: Record Demographic Information

Even if your products or services are targeted at a specific type of business, you'll communicate with the decision maker behind the business. In Step 2, record the demographic information of who makes the decisions (this could be the business owner, manager, or administrator) whom you want to serve in your Ideal Client Avatar worksheet. Demographic information includes the basic facts a person fills out about themselves on a census form. I've included a couple of examples for you.

Demographic Information on Ideal Clients for Bob Jackson:

Gender	Male or Female
Marital Status	Married or Widowed
Ethnicity	All
Job Titles	Mid- to late-career professionals such as:
	Operations Managers
	Teachers
	Engineers
	Small Business Owners
	Registered Nurses
	Government Employees
	Mid-level Corporate Professionals
Income	Household income of $75,000–$150,000 annually
Hobbies and Interests	Traveling (or planning to travel in retirement)
	Spending time with grandkids
	Golf, gardening, or walking groups
	Volunteering at church or in the community
	Reading about finance or watching market news
	Home improvement and DIY projects
	Health and wellness (many are focused on aging well)

Demographic Information on Ideal Clients for Maggie Abrams:

Gender	Primarily Female
Marital Status	Married, Single, or Divorced
Ethnicity	Any
Job Titles	Life Coach
	Health Coach
	Realtor
	Virtual Assistant
	Etsy Shop Owner
	Boutique Owner
	Online Educator
	Small Business Owner
	Creative Freelancer
	Service-Based Entrepreneur
Income	Business revenue from $40,000 to $150,000 annually
Hobbies and Interests	Listening to business and mindset podcasts
	Watching Instagram or TikTok for inspiration
	Online learning (courses, webinars, YouTube tutorials)
	Personal development books
	Content creation (or wanting to!)
	Networking in women's business groups on Facebook
	Planning for family vacations, girls' nights, or self-care routines
	Coffee, Canva, and content batching

Step 3: Problems and Dreams

Step 3 is where things start to get real. It's time to get into the nitty-gritty of what makes your ideal client avatar tick. You'll want to consider the following questions:

- What problem is your ideal client avatar dealing with? Think about the root issues that are causing the pain and discomfort your ideal client or customer is currently experiencing. Describe the problem in detail.
- How does that make them feel? Think about the "symptoms" the person you can help will have. What feelings and emotions are they experiencing?
- What is the ultimate goal or end result they want to achieve? If the problem is the nightmare scenario, then their ultimate goal is the dream. Paint the picture of what their lives could look like once their problem is solved.

You can always refine this later, but the answers to these questions will give you a starting point to think about the person you can help. On step 3 of your Ideal Client Avatar worksheet, record your answers to the following questions. I've included a couple of examples of what this might look like.

Bob Jackson's Client Avatar Questions:

What problem is your ideal client avatar dealing with?

They're approaching retirement and feeling uncertain about whether they're truly ready. They've been working hard for decades, have savings and maybe some investments, but they don't know how to turn what they've built into a sustainable income.

They're overwhelmed by financial decisions: when to take Social Security, how to handle healthcare costs, whether they need long-term care insurance, how to manage taxes, and knowing what to do if they'll outlive their money.

They're also worried about making mistakes that could jeopardize their future comfort or put a burden on their spouse or children.

How does that make them feel?

It makes them feel anxious and insecure. They're frustrated because they've done "all the right things" financially (worked hard and saved regularly) but still feel unsure. They may even feel embarrassed or ashamed that they don't understand how to piece it all together.

Some feel paralyzed by all the choices. Others are quietly panicking, worried that they waited too long to start planning. What they really want is clarity, confidence, and someone they can trust to walk them through the related issues.

What is the ultimate goal or end result they want to achieve?

They want to retire with peace of mind knowing their money will last, their spouse will be cared for, and they won't have to depend on their kids. They want a clear, simple plan they can trust—one that tells them exactly how to manage their money, make smart choices, and enjoy the next chapter of life without fear.

Ultimately, they want freedom.

Freedom from financial stress.

Freedom to travel or spend time with loved ones.

Freedom to enjoy the life they've worked hard for.

Next, let's look at these questions from Maggie's perspective.

Maggie Abram's Client Avatar Questions:

What problem is your ideal client avatar dealing with?
They're struggling to consistently engage on social media in a way that actually grows their business. They know video content is crucial, but they lack the time, creativity, or technical skills to produce high-quality and on-trend content that grabs attention and converts that attention into conversations with leads. They're often stuck staring at a blank screen, unsure of what to post, overwhelmed by trying to edit videos, keeping up with algorithm changes, and staying visible to their audience.
How does that make them feel?
They feel frustrated, stuck, and left behind. They see other business owners growing and feel like they're missing out on opportunities. There's a constant guilt that they "should be doing more," but they're already stretched thin running their business, managing family life, or juggling multiple roles. Many feel burned out, inconsistent, or insecure about how their brand is presented online.
What is the ultimate goal or end result they want to achieve?
They want to develop a strong, consistent online presence that attracts clients and builds their brand without spending all day creating content. They want polished, on-trend video content that reflects their personality and values, helps them stand out, and drives real results (more leads, more engagement, more revenue). Ultimately, they want their time back to focus on their business, spend time with their families, and stop stressing about social media.

By the time you've completed the Ideal Client Avatar worksheet, you'll have a well-rounded idea of your ideal clients and customers, as well as how the problem you can solve is affecting them. That's when you'll be ready to start setting up your first sales strategy. Congrats! If you need help getting clear on your ideal client avatar, I've provided some ChatGPT prompts in your Revenue Runway classroom that can help you brainstorm.

Now it's time to create your core sales message so you can start landing clients and generating income in chapter 10.

Chapter 10
Your Core Sales Message

Congratulations! You're just one step away from finishing your Revenue Runway Blueprint! Now you will create your core sales message: a clear statement of who you serve, what they want, and how you help them. In chapter 7.3, you learned why having a core sales message is important. Now let's create yours so that you never have to stumble or stammer over your words again when someone asks, "So, what do you do?"

Like I mentioned in chapter 7.3, there are only three main pieces of information you need to collect so that you can put your core sales message together:

- WHO you serve. This is your ideal client avatar.
- WHAT they want. This is the problem they have that you can solve; a problem they want to get rid of.
- HOW you serve them. This refers to the services you offer.

If you've completed your Irresistible Offer worksheets and your Ideal Client Avatar worksheets, you already have this information.

I've given you some examples of core sales message statements based on my own business and our fictional business owners, Bob Jackson and Maggie Abrams. You can read through the examples, then dive into the Core Sales Message worksheet from your Revenue Runway classroom. Fill in the blanks for your WHO, WHAT, and HOW to create your core sales message: *I help [WHO I serve] get [WHAT they want] by [HOW I serve them].*

Example 1: My Offer

Here's how I'd fill out the WHO, WHAT, and HOW for my own offer and audience:

WHO I serve:	Restoration cleaning company owners
WHAT they want:	Fully booked calendars
HOW I serve them:	Data-driven lead generation

Core Sales Message: I help restoration company owners achieve fully booked calendars by generating data-driven leads who schedule calls and make appointments.

Example 2: Bob Jackson

Here's how I'd fill it out for Bob, a financial advisor who helps professionals plan for retirement:

WHO I serve:	Professionals in their 50s and 60s
WHAT they want:	To retire with financial peace of mind
HOW I serve them:	I create custom retirement plans that work with their budgets and goals.

Core Sales Message: I help professionals in their 50s and 60s retire with financial peace of mind by creating custom retirement plans that align with their budgets and goals.

Example 3: Maggie Abrams

Here's how I'd fill it out for Maggie, a social media manager for online coaches and course creators:

WHO I serve:	Online coaches and course creators
WHAT they want:	To gain more clients
HOW I serve them:	I create social media content that grows their reach and engagement.

Core Sales Message: I help online coaches and course creators gain more clients through social media content that increases their reach and engagement.

Now It's Your Turn!

Fill in step 1 on your Core Sales Message worksheet with your WHO, WHAT, and HOW. Then plug your information into step 2, the framework of the Core Sales Message statement. Once you've done that, your Revenue Runway Blueprint is complete!

Congratulations! If you've made it this far, you've invested a ton of time and effort into your Revenue Runway. And this is only the beginning! Now it's time to finally take off. You're on your way to building a business that will generate income for you no matter what life throws your way, and you should be very proud of yourself.

You're not in this alone though! Keep reading to learn how you can access more resources and support in the conclusion.

Conclusion

If you've made it to this point in the book, let me be the first to say congratulations! I'm proud of you!

You didn't just read a book. You showed up for yourself. You stared down the chaos, the doubts, and the distractions and said, "I'm doing this anyway." That right there? That's exactly the kind of grit it takes to build a business when life isn't going according to plan. And now, because of that, you have something that so many people never get: a clear path forward.

You now have the tools, the clarity, and the framework to start or grow a business even in the middle of life's messiest and most uncertain moments. Let's take a moment to look at what you've accomplished inside this book.

What You've Learned

In part 1, I explained why you need a Revenue Runway. I shared some of my story with you, and I was honest about what it takes to launch during hard times. You learned:

- The best businesses are often born in the middle of a storm, not after it passes.
- Waiting for "perfect timing" is a myth and a trap.

- Taking messy, imperfect action is always better than standing still.
- Action alone isn't enough—clarity must come first.

In part 2, we traveled from roadblocks to the Revenue Runway. We tackled the most common issues that trip people up when trying to start a business. Then I revealed the Revenue Runway step by step. You discovered:

- The 3 Pillars of the Revenue Runway: Irresistible Offer, Ideal Client Avatar, and Sales Strategy.
- How to get out of your own way to build with confidence and not confusion
- Why most businesses fail before they ever get started, and how to avoid that by validating your offer before selling it.
- How to stay focused on what actually brings in revenue so you're not burning time on busy work.

In part 3, you got down to business. I showed you how to build your own unique Revenue Runway Blueprint. You were given the tools you needed to:

- Craft and validate your irresistible offer using real-world examples.
- Identify and connect with your ideal clients so you're clear on who you want to serve, what they want, and the problem they have that your offer can solve.
- Create a core sales message that attracts, engages, and converts without sounding pushy or fake.
- Inside the workbook, you were able to build your own Revenue Runway one manageable task at a time. Whether you're starting from scratch, rebuilding, or

scaling something already in motion, you now have a blueprint you can follow every single time life throws you a curveball.

What Comes Next

Now that you have the framework, it's time to take the leap. Don't wait for someday. Don't put things off until circumstances "feel right" or you have more time or confidence or permission.

It's your turn, and you don't have to do it alone. If you've reached the end of this book and you're thinking, "I get it, but I'd love help putting it into action," my team and I are here for you!

The Revenue Runway isn't just a book. It's a movement, a method, and a support system. And I'm ready to walk this journey with you. There are several ways to connect by visiting www.therevenuerunway.com. You can learn from or work with me through the following ways:

- Listen to my podcast, Revenue Runway. You'll find episodes on entrepreneurship and marketing that will help you start and grow your business.

- Book a strategy call. Log in to your private, personal Revenue Runway classroom at www.therevenuerunway.com to book a strategy call. I'll help you clarify your next step, get unstuck, and start moving toward a business that gives you the time, income, and freedom you've been craving.

- Join The Revenue Runway membership program. Want to link arms with other entrepreneurs and take action on your Revenue Runway Blueprint together? Inside The Revenue Runway membership program, you can!

No matter what's going on in your world right now, remember this:

You are capable.

You are resourceful.

And you are absolutely not alone.

I can't wait for your Revenue Runway dreams to take flight!

–Kalen

Resources

Your Revenue Runway Private Classroom

I've created the Revenue Runway Blueprint Workbook, a collection of downloadable worksheets and guides you can use to build your offer, target market, and sales messaging. These resources and more are available for you to use free of charge and have been loaded into a private classroom that can be accessed by visiting www.therevenuerunway.com.

Once there, you'll be prompted to create a free Revenue Runway account. This sets up a private, password-protected classroom where you can download all the free resources that come with this book.

About the Author

Kalen Marie Cotto is a fractional Chief Marketing Officer and the founder of KMC Digital, where she helps small businesses and startups transform marketing confusion into clarity and clarity into growth. Kalen is known for building straightforward strategies that actually drive leads, sales, and momentum.

Her superpower? Helping founders who are tired of spinning their wheels create marketing systems that work. Whether you're bootstrapped or fully backed, you don't have to stay stuck in "random acts of marketing." Kalen brings the structure, insight, and execution needed to move you forward without the bloated agency fees or generic playbooks.

Kalen's approach is grounded in real-world experience. Before founding KMC Digital, she served in the US military coordinating media in high-stakes combat zones. Working alongside journalists like Lara Logan and Oliver North during her deployment in Iraq, she learned how to deliver powerful messages under pressure, stay mission-focused, and lead teams with clarity. Today, she brings that same discipline to the world of entrepreneurship. She cuts through the noise to help business owners tell better stories and reach the right audience at the right time.

KMC Digital offers services like search intent strategy, lead generation audits, email re-engagement campaigns, and full-funnel builds. Kalen acts as her clients' part-time CMO—their partner in scaling, not just their marketing help. She's the one founders call when they need clear messaging, focused strategy, and someone who actually understands the chaos of building something from the ground up.

She's also a HighLevel power user, so if you're trying to wrangle your CRM, automate follow-ups, or finally fix your leaky sales pipeline, she's got the tech chops to back the strategy.

Kalen's clients love her straight-shooter style, tactical mindset, and uncanny ability to "just get it." She's been called part marketer, part operator, and part therapist because running a business is personal and growth isn't just about numbers, it's about leadership.

Whether you're pre-revenue and scrappy or managing a lean team and trying to scale efficiently, Kalen is the strategic growth partner who shows up with honesty, heart, and strategy—a playbook that fits the stage you're in.

If you're ready to stop guessing at your marketing and start building something that lasts, Kalen's the partner you want in your corner.

Made in the USA
Coppell, TX
24 February 2026

72257936R00095